KOKOMO-HOWARD COUNTY PUBLIC LIBRARY
www.kokomo.lib.in.us

KOKOMO-HOWARD COUNTY PUBLIC LIBRARY
KOKOMO, INDIANA

3 9223 033528467

Prairie Quilts

Projects for the Home Inspired by the Life and Times of Laura Ingalls Wilder

by Johanna Wilson

D1569268

©2004 Johanna Wilson
Published by

An imprint of F+W Publications, Inc.

700 East State Street • Iola, WI 54990-0001
715-445-2214 • 888-457-2873
www.krause.com

Our toll-free number to place an order or obtain a free catalog is 800-258-0929.

All rights reserved. No portion of this publication may be reproduced or transmitted in any form
or by any means, electronic or mechanical, including photocopy, recording, or any information
storage and retrieval system, without permission in writing from the publisher, except by a
reviewer who may quote brief passages in a critical article or review to be printed in a magazine
or newspaper, or electronically transmitted on radio or television.

Library of Congress Catalog Number: 2004100736

ISBN: 0-87349-773-2

Edited by Nicole Gould
Designed by Sharon Laufenberg

Printed in the United States of America

Dedication

To my family and friends who continue to encourage and support my creative endeavors. They have learned more about quilts, fabrics, and history than they ever thought they needed to know!

Especially to Joni, who asked when, not if, I was going to write a quilt book about Laura; to Ormon who asked, "Why not?"; and to Sandy and Carol who said, "Of course, you can."

Acknowledgments

Thanks to the twenty-first century quilters, Bonnie Erickson, Kathy Goral, Bev Keltgen, and Karla Schulz, who helped make new quilts for *Prairie Quilts*. Thanks to Julie Clark, Niki Gould, Ann Grefe, Carol Haines, Kristi Sotona, and Sandra Schaeffer for sharing quilts.

My sincerest respect and appreciation to the nineteenth- and twentieth-century quilters who left vintage blocks, quilt tops, and quilts for us to enjoy. I like to think they would be pleased to see their unfinished pieces turned into projects for this book. It has been a most rewarding process.

Thanks to Dan River for fabrics used in the Sister's Choice projects, and to Morning Glory and Mountain Mist for the batting used in many of the quilts.

Thanks to the staff at Krause, especially my editor Niki Gould, for their enthusiasm and guidance throughout this project.

Much appreciation goes to photographer Bob Best for his beautiful photography and willingness to try any shot.

Finally, thank you to the following for providing the locations for many of the photos in this book: Bob Strand and the Iola Historical Society, the Laura Ingalls Wilder Museum in Walnut Grove, and Joe and Tricia Kertzman.

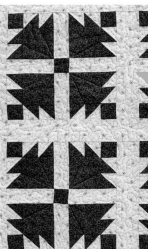

Table of Contents

Welcome to Prairie Quilts

Dear Reader,

In the 1870s, a little girl named Laura Ingalls lived with her family in a dugout home and played among the plum thickets along the banks of Plum Creek on the Minnesota prairie. As an adult, Laura Ingalls Wilder would write a series of wonderful books about her pioneer family's experiences as they moved around the country seeking a better life.

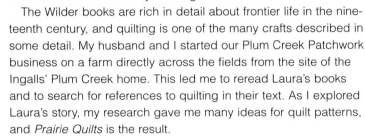

The Wilder books are rich in detail about frontier life in the nineteenth century, and quilting is one of the many crafts described in some detail. My husband and I started our Plum Creek Patchwork business on a farm directly across the fields from the site of the Ingalls' Plum Creek home. This led me to reread Laura's books and to search for references to quilting in their text. As I explored Laura's story, my research gave me many ideas for quilt patterns, and *Prairie Quilts* is the result.

In addition to the quilt blocks mentioned in the books, I searched for blocks that would typically have been used in the late nineteenth century. The opportunity to include time-appropriate vintage quilt blocks and quilt tops in this collection was especially rewarding. Several of the antique tops used in this book have been quilted by hand or by machine without major adjustments. Others were labors of love that required substantial effort in taking the quilts apart, resizing them, and sewing them back together. Some of the appliqué projects are especially delightful in their reflection of Laura's whimsical spirit.

I was particularly pleased to be able to complete some of the vintage quilt patterns with fabrics of my own design—thus linking past and present in a common effort. These projects have given me a greater appreciation for the work of early quilters and the rich heritage they have handed down to us.

This book has provided me with the opportunity to share that heritage with you and combine it with new fabrics using modern techniques. It is my hope that this collection of 27 projects will encourage you to explore your fabric collection and make a quilt reminiscent of the life Laura describes in her books. Perhaps it will pique your interest in rereading the Wilder books or, better still, lead you to share them with a child. You may also be enticed to visit one or more of the many Laura sites listed on page 128. However you choose to enhance your experience of the series, I wish you happy quilting and a rich journey through history.

— *Johanna Wilson*

Quilt Beginnings

Fabric Selection

Choosing fabric for your next quilt project should be an exhilarating experience, but I know many of you are uncomfortable with the prospect of making fabric choices. You may consider it an intimidating, but necessary, chore before you can begin the part you like best—making a quilt. Perhaps the following suggestions will offer you confidence to make fabric shopping more enjoyable.

❖ Choose one fabric you really like.

❖ Choose other fabrics that blend with the first.

❖ Vary the size (scale) of the prints.

❖ Try to visualize the fabrics as they will appear in the quilt (size, position).

❖ Consider including a new color, a plaid, a stripe, or a large print that may introduce just the sparkle you were hoping to find.

❖ Choose the best fabrics you can afford.

Design Area

Try to locate an area in your house where you can spread your fabrics or blocks out and step back. The bottom of a stairway works well as does a wall covered with cotton batting or flannel. If a wall is not available, you might cover a door or a large, flat piece of cardboard. You will find viewing the fabrics from a distance will make fabric choices obvious.

Accuracy

Be sure you have your sewing machine in good working order and proper lighting in all the areas where you will be working.

Have your cutting table the proper height to maintain a healthy back.

Find the rotary cutter that works best for you. ALWAYS close the blade when not in use.

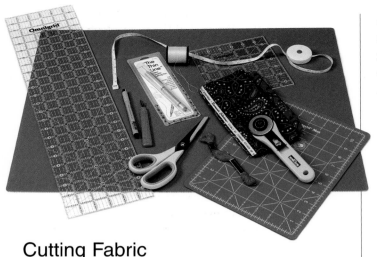

Cutting Fabric

Wouldn't Laura have loved our quilting tools? Cutting strips instead of individual squares to make nine-patches would have delighted her. Most of the quilts made at that time were made from scraps, not yardage, so the cutting process was tedious. One has only to notice the small, seamed-together pieces in a quilt block to realize how limited they were in fabric options. Each piece was precious.

We have a number of tools for cutting and measuring to make our tasks easier. Learning to use them to their best advantage is vital for good results in our quilts. Once you find the rulers and cutters you prefer, always use the same ones in the project you are making. There may be slight differences in tools that will affect the size.

As you cut strips across of the fabric, always cut away from your body. Stop cutting when you reach where your hand is holding the ruler, move your hand up several inches on the ruler, then continue cutting to the end of the strip. Not moving your hand puts extra pressure on the end of the ruler, causing the cutter to move the ruler and making the cut wider at the end. This happens when we are in a hurry or are cutting the last available fabric!

While all rotary blades can cause injury, dull ones do not cut fabric well. Replace your blades often, storing the used blades in a container, just for that purpose, to be disposed of in a safe manner.

Quarter-Inch Seams

Quilt patterns require a scant ¼" seam allowance. Check your accuracy by cutting three pieces 1½" x 4" and sewing them together along the 4" side. Press the seams to one side. Lay a ruler over the strips on the right-hand side to check the size. Your piece should measure 3½" across with the center strip measuring exactly 1". If it doesn't, cut new strips, adjust the seams, and repeat until you have found your correct measurement. Even if your machine has a ¼" foot, check the seam allowance the same way. You may be able to change the needle position to make adjustments. Mark your perfect seam allowance on the machine with a marking pen or a piece of tape. Always use this guide when sewing quilt seams. Painters' masking tape or black electrical tape will not leave a residue on your machine.

Pressing

Press pieces flat after each seam is sewn. Open the pieces, holding the darker side in one hand so that the lighter side, including the seam, is flat on the pressing board. Place the iron on the right side along the seam line, and hold it in place for a few seconds. This will automatically press the seam toward the darker fabric. Pick up the iron and put it down until you have reached the end of the seam. Remember to press, not iron, the pieces. Ironing is moving the iron in a back and forth motion, which can easily distort small pieces of fabric. Pressing from the right side helps avoid pressing pleats into the seam and distorting the size. Trim as necessary.

Trimming

Check the size of your pieced blocks as you press. The sizes for the pieces are given in parentheses, for example (2½" x 4½"), as you proceed through the patterns. Check the size after you press, and square up the block if necessary. Trimming to size will help keep the pieces square as you sew to the next piece, eliminating excess frustration! Check the seam allowance frequently.

Un-Sewing or Ripping Out

Occasionally, a seam may be too large, or we may sew the pieces together incorrectly which leads to reverse manual sewing, better known as ripping or un-sewing.

To un-sew, use a sharp seam ripper and carefully cut every third or fourth stitch along one side of the seam to be removed. Turn to the other side of the seam and gently lift the uncut thread with the dull side of the ripper. You should be able to loosen the entire seam.

If your stitches are very close together, you might want to adjust your stitch length on the sewing machine. Very small stitches are more difficult to rip out!

Basic Quilting Techniques

Basic quilting techniques used throughout the book are explained in this section. They may be used as a reference for unfamiliar techniques or to brush up on familiar techniques as you read through the pattern directions.

Strip Piecing

The invention of the rotary cutter introduced a quick and easy method of cutting strips the width of the fabric (WOF). Strip piecing is used for piecing the blocks and alternate blocks in many of the quilts.

1. Cut the strips the size indicated in the pattern. Place the strips right sides together and sew seam along the long side. Press toward the darker fabric.

2. Cut pieces from the strips, the size indicated, to be used in blocks.

3. Rearrange the cut segments and sew them together to make the blocks.

Half-Square Triangles

To increase accuracy in making half-square triangles, I like to make the half-square triangle larger than called for and then trim it to the size indicated in the pattern.

1. Place the strips of fabric with right sides together.

2. Cut squares from both strips at the same time, making them the size indicated in the pattern.

3. Cut the pairs of squares in half diagonally. Chain stitch the pairs of triangles along the bias edge, feeding them into the sewing machine one pair after the other without cutting the thread.

4. Press the triangles flat as they come from the machine, then cut the triangles apart.

5. Open the triangles right-side up and press toward the darker fabric, as described in the pressing section.

6. Trim each square using the rotary cutter and a small acrylic ruler. My choice of ruler is a small 6" square

with a 45-degree angle printed diagonally on the ruler. Place the diagonal of the ruler along the seam, with the fabric right-side up. Trim two sides of the half-square triangle with the rotary cutter. For accuracy, be sure the diagonal corner of the ruler is on the seam line. Placing the weight of your hand near the edge of the ruler will keep the fabric from creeping out as you cut.

7. Reposition the ruler on the other end of the diagonal seam and trim the sides to the required measurement. Trim all four sides.

8. Another method of making half-square triangles is to mark the diagonal on the squares and then sew a seam ¼" to each side of the diagonal. Press and trim to the desired size.

Note: If you have another method of making half-square triangles that is accurate, feel free to use it to make the half-squares the size indicated in each pattern. Many of us find trimming to size makes up for slight inaccuracies in cutting, piecing, and pressing. Use whatever method is most accurate for you.

Setting Triangles

Quilts with blocks set on point use triangles at the end of the diagonal rows to "square up" the rows. Triangles are made from squares cut twice on the diagonal. The triangles are lined up even with one edge of the row so that the triangle extends beyond the blocks at the other end. After the rows are sewn together, the edges are trimmed ¼" beyond the corners of the blocks.

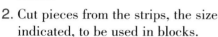

Blocks may use this same method, as in House that Pa Built (page 64) and Bachelor's Puzzle (page 76).

The triangles at the corners of a quilt with blocks set on point are made from squares cut once on the diagonal. The triangles are centered on the end of the row. Find the center of the bias side by folding the bias side of the triangle, wrong sides together, and pinching at the fold. Find the center of the end block by folding the edge with right sides together. Match the creases with right sides together. The triangle will fall into the crease on the block. Pin in place. Stitch the pieces together with the triangle on the bottom to avoid stretching when sewing. This is the method used in the quilts with blocks set on point.

Flip Corners

Sewing along the diagonal of the small square allows you to create a triangle without cutting the fabric on the diagonal, thus avoiding possible distortion.

There are several methods of marking the diagonal line for sewing. Try each and decide which way works best for you. You can chain sew all the pieces with any of these methods.

Method 1: Draw a line from corner to corner with a marking pen or sharp pencil. Hold the ruler firmly to avoid rippling. Stitch on the line.

Method 2: Fold and press the diagonal of the square with wrong sides together. Place the square on the fabric to be sewn with the diagonal in the correct direction. Sew in the ditch created by the fold.

Method 3: Mark a guide line on the bed of your machine with a fine permanent pen or a piece of tape directly in front of the needle. Make this line as long as possible. This method allows you to sew the diagonal without marking or folding each one. Begin sewing the diagonal with one corner of the square under the needle and the opposite corner on the line drawn with the permanent pen. Stitch the seam, guiding the opposite corner of the square along the drawn line. If your machine wants to "eat" the corner as you feed it in, put a scrap of fabric in the machine before beginning to sew diagonals.

To stabilize the piece, I like to trim the back of the inner triangle only, leaving the background piece as a guide for sewing the next piece. Press all the pieces flat as they come from the machine. Fold the square over the background piece, and press along the seam line. Use the method that gives you the best results.

Single Flip Corners

(one triangle)

Using pieces the size indicated in the pattern, sew a square on the diagonal in the direction indicated. Trim the inner triangle, press flat, fold over the background piece, and press again.

Double Flip Corners

(two triangles)

Using pieces the size indicated in the pattern, sew a square on the diagonal in the direction indicated.

Follow the steps for Single Flip Corners including

pressing. Sew a second square as noted in the pattern. Be sure the angle of the second square matches the illustration.

Double-Double Flip Corners

(four triangles)

Using pieces the size indicated in the pattern, sew a square on the diagonal in the direction indicated.

Follow the steps for Single Flip Corners including pressing. Sew a second square on the opposite corner and repeat the procedure. Trim and press. Repeat with the last two corners.

Stem Stitch

Embroidery stitches are used in several of the quilts. The stem stitch can be used for the Redwork Pillow Shams (page 34), Light in the Window (page 57), and Give Us Our Daily Bread (page 114). Stitching can be used as embellishment on Flowers for Ma (page 36), Prairie Queen (page 91), and Prairie Rose (page 116).

Happy quilters proudly show off blocks made at the author's annual retreat.

Pillow Backs

1. Cut two fabric pieces for the pillow backs, according to the directions. Fold each piece in half, wrong sides together. Stitch ⅜" from the fold to secure the edge of each piece.

2. Lay one folded back on top of the other, overlapping the folded edges to equal the measurement of the pillow top. Lay the quilted pillow top right-side up on the back pieces. Pin the two layers together to hold the pieces while stitching around the pieces with a scant ¼" basting stitch.

3. Complete the pillow by sewing your binding of choice around the edge. Finish as you finish a quilt (see Finishing, page 12). Insert the appropriate pillow form or stuffing. Slipstitching the edge is optional.

Signature Blocks

Method 1: Press the shiny side of freezer paper to the wrong side of the block to be signed. This will stabilize the fabric for signing with a permanent fabric pen. After the blocks are signed, press with a hot iron to set the ink. Remove the freezer paper before sewing the blocks together.

Method 2: If the blocks are to be signed after quilt construction, press the shiny side of a square of freezer paper to the back of each signature block. Cut the paper the scant size of the block (3½" for a 4" finished block). Use permanent fabric pens for signing. Press to set the ink. Remove the paper. Piece as usual.

Ormon waiting patiently for the wind to stop blowing so he can snap a picture of the Legacy quilt. (See page 16.)

Quilt Endings

Borders

A variety of borders are included in this book. The length of each border is determined after the quilt top is pieced. There is no reason to actually measure the border pieces.

Plain Borders

See Bear Tracks in the Berry Patch, page 47.

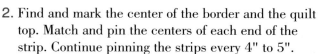

1. Carefully lay strips of border fabric lengthwise across the center of the quilt. Smooth any wrinkles. Cut two lengthwise borders.

2. Find and mark the center of the border and the quilt top. Match and pin the centers of each end of the strip. Continue pinning the strips every 4" to 5".

3. Sew the lengthwise borders to the quilt. Press toward the border.

4. Lay strips of border fabric crosswise across the center of the quilt and cut two crosswise borders.

5. Find and mark the center of the border and quilt top. Match and pin the centers and each end of the strip. Continue pinning the strips every 4" to 5".

6. Sew the crosswise borders to the sides of the quilt. Press toward the border.

7. Quilts may have more than one border. Repeat the sequence for each border.

Borders with Blocks or Squares in the Corners

See Bachelor's Puzzle, page 76.

1. Lay strips of border fabric lengthwise across the center of the quilt. Cut to size. Set aside.

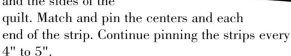
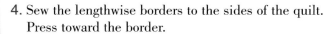

2. Lay strips of border fabric crosswise across the center of the quilt. Cut to size. Set aside.

3. Find and mark the center of the lengthwise border pieces and the sides of the quilt. Match and pin the centers and each end of the strip. Continue pinning the strips every 4" to 5".

4. Sew the lengthwise borders to the sides of the quilt. Press toward the border.

5. Sew blocks or squares to each end of the crosswise borders. Press toward the border.

6. Find and mark the center of the crosswise border pieces and sides of the quilt. Match and pin the seams.

7. Sew the crosswise borders in place. Press toward the border.

Finishing

Quilting

Hand quilting designs may be marked on your quilt before layering. You may also use the quilt pieces for stitching guides. Test all markers before using them. If you prefer to have your quilt machine stitched, seek out an electric needle specialist. Ask to see a sample of work and the name of a satisfied customer before leaving your quilt.

Quilt Backs

The machine quilter will tell you how much larger to prepare the back. Our backs have 4" added to the back measurements. I often use leftover pieces for the back. An extra block or two creates a pleasant and unexpected surprise when included on the back. See the Scrap Bag Quilt on page 60.

For a quilt up to 75" long, I use one crosswise seam. Measure the quilt crosswise, add six to this number, and then double the number. Divide the total by 36 to figure the yardage to purchase for the back.

For a quilt more then 75" wide and less than 75" long, I use one lengthwise seam. Measure the quilt lengthwise, add six to this number, and then double the number. Divide the total by 36 to figure the yardage to purchase for the back.

For quilts larger than 75", I use two seams. Measure the shortest side, add six to this number, and then multiply by three. Divide by 36 to figure the yardage to purchase for the back.

Press the pieces and open seams before sandwiching the quilt.

Quilt Sandwich

Sandwich your quilt by placing the back right-side down on a flat surface. A large table will save your back. Quilt shops often have classrooms available to use for this purpose. Church tables pushed together are another suggestion. For the more agile quilter, the floor may be a possibility.

Secure the top edge of the quilt back to the flat surface with masking tape or with clips. Place the batting and the quilt top, right-side up, on top of the backing. Smooth each to remove wrinkles. Baste every 3" to 4" with safety pins, basting thread, or a quilt tack device. Use safety pins if you are quilting on your sewing machine.

Quilt as desired by hand or by machine.

Wild plums growing along Plum Creek.

Quilt Hanger

For ease in hanging, a quilt sleeve or hanger can be attached.

1. Cut a strip 6" wide and 1" shorter than the width of the quilt. Turn and press under ¼" at each short end. Turn again and stitch.

2. Fold the strip in half lengthwise, with wrong sides together. Press.

3. Machine baste the hanger to the back of the quilt, matching raw edges of the quilt with the hanger at the top.

4. Pin and hand stitch the hanger to the quilt back so that the fold is ¼" above the bottom of the hanger, leaving fabric to fit around the rod and remain flat on the front of the quilt.

Note: I like to use flat "screen" molding, available in lumber yards, for a hanger. It is inexpensive and can easily be cut to any size you wish. Small quilts can be held up with large head pins pushed into wallboard at an angle or with push pins.

Binding

The final step in finishing your quilt is to attach the binding.

1. Trim the backing and batting even with the top. Baste ¼" from the outer edge of the quilt to hold the layers and keep them from slipping as the binding is applied. A walking foot makes sewing the binding easier.

2. Binding is usually cut crosswise across the width of the fabric. I use 2½" wide binding strips for small quilts and often increase the width to 2¾" for bed quilts.

Tip: If I am using a stripe or a plaid for the binding, I cut the pieces on the bias. You may notice that many of my quilts have striped, plaid, or checked bindings. I encourage you to try them also. They add sparkle to a quilt. Remember to allow for additional fabric if you are cutting your binding strips on the bias.

3. Sew the binding strips, right sides together, at right angles as if mitering them, to create the length indicated in the pattern. Fold the binding strip in half lengthwise with wrong sides together. Press.

4. Pin the binding to the right side of one side of the quilt every 4" to 5", matching the edges and leaving a 10" tail.

5. Sew to ¼" of the first corner. Remove the quilt from the machine. Miter the corners by folding the binding at right angles, perpendicular to the direction of the sewn seam. Refold the binding back on itself so the second fold is even with the edge of the next side of the quilt to be sewn.

6. Pin and sew the binding to the next corner and repeat mitering the corners until all sides are sewn, leaving a second 10" tail unsewn.

7. Overlap the binding edges and cut one end longer than the other, exactly the width of the cut binding. With the quilt toward you, open the binding and place the right end of the binding over the left end, right sides together at right angles. Pin. Sew on the diagonal, corner to corner. Check to see that seam is correct, trim the seam, press, and complete sewing on the binding.

8. Turn the folded edge of the binding to the back of the quilt, covering the stitching line, and slipstitch it in place with thread to match the binding.

9. Admire your quilt!

Labels

Always sign and date your quilt. Future generations deserve to know who created this masterpiece.

1. Use a permanent fabric pen to sign the quilt back or create a personal label for the quilt.

2. To make a label, stabilize it by pressing the shiny side of freezer paper to the back of the label fabric.

3. Write your name, address, date, and other pertinent information about the quilt on the label with permanent fabric pens. Embellish as you wish.

4. Press to set the ink. Remove the freezer paper, turn under the edges, and hand stitch the label to the quilt.

It is a good idea to check any previously completed quilts for labels. It is never too late to add one. Imagine the pleasure someone will have in the future when he or she finds one of your signed quilts in a trunk!

Little House in the Big Woods

This story tells of the adventures of the Ingalls family as they homestead in their log house in the woods of western Wisconsin. In the fall, they butcher the hog and store vegetables in the attic in preparation for winter. In the evenings, they listen to Pa's stories and his fiddle music. There is a sugaring off party at Grandpa's with the cousins where everyone enjoys Grandma's maple sugar and dancing to Pa's fiddle. The Big Woods Quilt is a sampler of quilt blocks representing the Ingalls family from the mind's eye of Laura as a child.

Pieced by Karla Schultz
Machine quilted by Bonnie Erickson
82" x 88"

Big Woods Legacy Quilt

A long time ago, a little girl named Laura lived in the Big Woods of Wisconsin with her Ma and Pa and big sister, Mary.

Materials

Yardage	Fabric
3⅛ yd.	A - Outer border - focus fabric (red paisley)
3 yd.	B - Inner border, blocks, binding (navy)
1¼ yd.	C - Setting triangles, blocks (tan)
1¾ yd.	D - Light background, setting triangles, blocks
1 yd.	E - Block border and blocks (tan)
¾ yd.	F - Blocks (green paisley)
¾ yd.	G - Blocks (tan)
¼ yd.	H - Blocks (red plaid)
¾ yd.	I - Center border and blocks (tan plaid)
⅓ yd.	J - Blocks (light blue)
⅞ yd.	K - Blocks (dark blue)
⅜ yd.	L - Blocks (red)
Fat quarter	M - Blocks, optional (green)
Fat quarter	N - Blocks, optional (green)

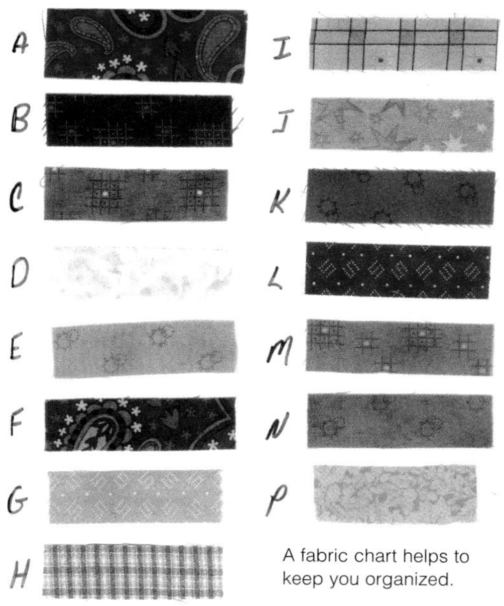

A fabric chart helps to keep you organized.

Cutting Directions

Cut in the order listed for the best use of the fabric.

❖ From **Fabric A** Red Paisley, cut:

Outer Border

(4) 8½" x 82"* lengthwise strips
*Will be trimmed when piecing is completed.

Tree Border

(4) 6½" x 22½" WOF (Width of Fabric) strips

❖ From **Fabric B** Navy Tic Tack Toe, cut:

Border #2

(8) 3½" strips x WOF
(1) 8½" strip x WOF into:
    (4) 8½" squares

Tree

(3) 3" strips x WOF
(6) 2½" squares

Kitchen Wood Box

(24) 2½" squares

Oh, Susannah!

(2) 2½" strips x WOF into:
    (16) 2½" x 4½" rectangles

❖ From **Fabric C** Tan Tic Tack Toe, cut:

Setting triangles and rectangles

(4) 9½" squares
(2) 6½" strip x WOF into:
    (4) 6½" x 10½"

Bear Track

(1) 2½" strip x WOF

Tree Trunk

(1) 3¼" x 18" rectangle

Kitchen Wood Box

(3) 1½" strips x WOF into:
    (12) 1½" x 2½"
    (12) 1½" x 4½"

Fence

(2) 1½" strips x WOF into:
    (12) 1½" x 4½"
(2) 1" strips x WOF into:
    (2) 1" x 28"

❖ From **Fabric D** Tan Background, cut:

Setting Triangles

(1) 17" square
(1) 12½" square

Tree

(3) 3" strips x WOF

Sister's Choice

(1) 3" strip x WOF
(1) 2½" strip x WOF into:
    (1) 2½" x 21" strip
    (8) 2½" squares

Bear Track

(4) 6½" squares
(1) 2½" strip x WOF
(4) 2" squares

Yard

(2) 4½" strips x WOF into:
    (4) 4½" x 10½" rectangles
    (4) 5½" x 4½" rectangles
    (3) 1½" x 28" strips

❖ From **Fabric E** Medium Tan, cut:

Path through the Woods

(2) 7½" squares

Snail's Trail

(2) 5½" squares
(4) 4½" squares
(4) 3½" squares
(4) 2½" squares
(1) 1½" x 14" strip

❖ From **Fabric F** Green Paisley, cut:

Bear Track

(4) 5" squares

Tree

(1) 6½" square
(1) 3¾" square

Path through the Woods

(2) 7½" squares

Cutting Directions (Continued)

Snail's Trail
(6) 5½" squares
(4) 4½" squares
(4) 3½" squares
(4) 2½" squares
(1) 1½" x 14" strip

Leaf Appliqué – optional

❖ From **Fabric G** Tan S, cut:

Tree Background
(2) 7" squares
(1) 6½" square
(2) 4½" x 8½" rectangles
(4) 2½" border strips x WOF
(3) 2½" squares

Kitchen Wood Box
(3) 1½" strips x WOF into:
    (12) 1½" x 4½"
    (12) 1½" x 6½"

Stars
Scrap for moon (pattern on page 28)

❖ From **Fabric H** Red Plaid, cut:

Oh, Susannah!
(1) 2½" strip x WOF
(16) 2½" squares

❖ From **Fabric I** Tan Plaid, cut:

Border #1
(8) 2½" strips x WOF

Kitchen Wood Box
(6) 2½" squares

❖ From **Fabric J** Blue Star, cut:

Stars
(2) 3" strips x WOF
(10) 2½" squares

❖ From **Fabric K** Dark Blue, cut:

Star Background
(2) 3" strips x WOF
(3) 2½" strips x WOF into:
    (2) 2½" x 10½"
    (40) 2½" squares
(2) 6½" strips x WOF into:
    (7) 6½" x 4½"
    (6) 6½" x 2½"
    (1) 4½" x 10½"

❖ From **Fabric L** Red S, cut:

Sister's Choice
(1) 3" strip x WOF
(2) 2½" strips x WOF into:
    (1) 2½" x 21" strip

(10) 2½" squares

Oh, Susannah!
(1) 2½" strip x WOF

❖ From **Fabric M** Green Tic Tack Toe, cut:

Leaf Appliqué – optional (pattern on page 28)

❖ From **Fabric N** Green, cut:

Leaf Appliqué – optional (pattern on page 28)

❖ **WOF** indicates that you should cut the strip the full width of the fabric.

❖ For ease in identification, label all cut fabric and place in zip lock bags by block name, for example: Tree, Stars, Bear Tracks, etc.

❖ There are several scrappy blocks that you will be cutting from your scraps: Log Cabin, Path through the Woods, and Leaf Appliqué (optional).

Tree

This traditional Tree block represents the Ingalls family as well as their location in the Big Woods. Laura's story explains how the bears search the bee tree for honey; how Pa climbs a tree to wait for deer, and then watches them instead of bringing home meat for the family; how a hollow tree works as a smokehouse for preserving meat by smoking it; and how trees provide heat for the log cabin.

Trunk Unit

1. Cut the 6½" F and G squares in half diagonally. Sew an F and G triangle together along the short side. (Bias edges are exposed! Handle carefully.) Make one and one reversed.

2. Sew a 4½" x 8½" G rectangle to the bias side of both G triangles.

3. Cut the 3¾" F square in half diagonally. Match

the centers of the F triangle and the end of G rectangle. Sew the bias edge of an F triangle to the bottom of both G rectangles.

4. Sew one section to each side of the 3¼" x 18" C trunk fabric matching the bottom edges.

5. Cut a 7" fabric G square in half diagonally. Center and sew the bias edge of one triangle to the bottom of the trunk.

6. Find the center of the trunk by laying the diagonal of a large square ruler lengthwise on the center of the trunk and measuring 7¼" from the center in all directions. Trim the tree trunk unit to measure 14½".

Half-Square Triangles

Review Half-Square Triangles, page 9.

1. Place the 3" strips of Fabric B and D right sides together. Press.

2. Cut 3" squares from both strips at the same time. Make 18 pairs.

3. Cut each pair diagonally once. Sew triangles together with a ¼" seam along the bias edge.

4. Feed the triangles through the machine one after the other without cutting the thread. Press, then cut the triangles apart. Make 36 triangle squares. Trim to 2½".

5. Sew three rows of four half-square triangles. Sew a 2½" B square to the light triangle at the end of the first row.

6. Sew a 2½" B square and one half-square triangle to the light triangle at the end of the second row.

7. Sew a 2½" B square and two half-square triangles to the light triangles at the end of the third row. Sew the 3 rows together.

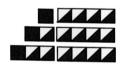

8. Repeat Steps 5 to 7, reversing the triangle squares so they are pointing in the opposite direction.

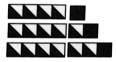

9. Lay a ruler on the right-hand side of the 2½" B squares and trim ¼" beyond the seam line at 45 degrees. Repeat for the reversed set. Mark the centers.

10. Cut a 7" Fabric G square in half diagonally and mark the center of the bias edge.

11. Match the centers of a Fabric G triangle to the center of each pieced unit. Trim each to measure 6½" x 14½".

12. Sew one unit to the left side of the trunk unit with dark triangles facing the trunk.

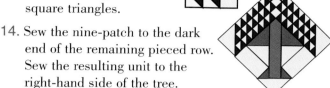

13. Make a nine-patch from the 2½" fabric G squares and remaining half-square triangles.

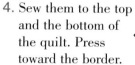

14. Sew the nine-patch to the dark end of the remaining pieced row. Sew the resulting unit to the right-hand side of the tree.

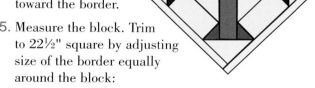

15. Press the block carefully and check its size. The tree should measure 20½". If your block is less than the desired size, the next border will compensate when it is trimmed.

Block Borders

Note: Borders were cut 2½" to allow for variance in tree block measurement (fudge factor).

1. Measure and cut two fabric G borders the length at the center of the quilt.

2. Sew to opposite sides of the tree. Press toward border.

3. Measure and cut two borders the width at the center of the quilt.

4. Sew them to the top and the bottom of the quilt. Press toward the border.

5. Measure the block. Trim to 22½" square by adjusting size of the border equally around the block:

   Find and mark the center of the trunk by folding the tree in quarters. Position a large square ruler lengthwise along the trunk with 11¼" on the center mark. Trim two sides 11¼". Reposition the ruler at the center crosswise on the trunk and trim the other two sides at 11¼" (22½" x 22½").

6. Set the Tree block aside until all the blocks are completed.

Bear Tracks

Encounters with bears are numerous in the Big Woods. A bear robbing a honey tree is chased away by Pa, leaving the honey cache for him to take home. Ma and Laura are frightened by a bear in the corral when they go to milk the cow that remains safe inside the barn. Pa has many bear tales, too.

Half-Square Triangles

Review Half-Square Triangles, page 9.

1. Place the 2½" strips of C and D fabric with right sides together.

2. Cut 2½" squares from both strips at the same time. Cut 12 pairs.

3. Cut the squares diagonally once. Sew the triangles together with a ¼" seam along the bias edge.

4. Feed the triangles through the machine one after the other without cutting the thread. Press, then cut the triangles apart. Make 24 half-square triangles. Trim to 2".

Piecing

1. Sew three half-square triangles together in a row. Make four strips. Note the orientation of the triangles (2" x 5").

2. Sew a row of triangles to each 5" fabric F square with the dark triangles toward the square. Make four.

3. Sew three half-square triangles together in a row. Make four strips (2" x 5"). Note that the orientation is reversed.

4. Sew a 2" Fabric D square to the dark triangle at the end of each strip.

5. Sew a triangle strip to the side of each Fabric F square as shown. Note the orientation of the toes (6½" x 6½").

6. Sew a 6½" background square D to the side of the pieced block as shown. Make four pairs (6½" x 12½").

7. Sew the pairs together, alternating blocks. Make two (12½" x 12½").

8. Set the Bear Tracks blocks aside until all the blocks are completed.

Sister's Choice

The three Ingalls sisters, Mary, Laura, and Carrie are represented by Sister's Choice.

Half-Square Triangles

1. Place the 3" strips of fabrics D and L right sides together. Press.

2. Cut 3" squares from both strips at the same time. Cut eight pairs.

3. Cut the squares diagonally once. Sew the triangles together with a ¼" seam along the bias edge.

4. Feed the triangles through the machine one after the other without cutting the thread. Press, then cut the triangles apart. Make 16 half-square triangles. Trim to 2½".

Piecing

1. Sew a half-square triangle and a 2½" fabric D square together. Make eight pairs (2½" x 4½").

2. Sew a half-square triangle and a 2½" fabric L square together. Make eight pairs (2½" x 4½").

3. Sew the pairs together as shown. Make eight (4½" x 4½").

4. Sew the 21" strips of fabrics D and L together along the long edge. Press toward the dark and cut at 2½" intervals. Make eight cuts.

5. Sew a 2½" fabric D and L cut between half-square triangle blocks, alternating colors as shown. Make four (4½" x 10½").

6. Sew a 2½" fabric L square between two pairs of squares, alternating colors. Make two.

7. Arrange and sew the rows together. Make two (10½" x 10½").

8. Set the Sister's Choice blocks aside until all blocks are completed.

Stars

The stars were shining faintly through the trees in the Big Woods as Ma and Laura went to the barn to milk the cow.

Half-Square Triangles

1. Place the 3" strips of fabrics J and K right sides together. Press.

2. Cut 3" squares from both strips at the same time. Cut 20 pairs.

3. Cut the squares diagonally once. Sew the triangles together with a ¼" seam along the bias edge.

4. Feed the triangles through the machine one after the other without cutting the thread. Press, then cut the triangles apart. Make 40 half-square triangles. Trim to 2½".

Piecing

1. Sew a 2½" fabric K square to each side of a half-square triangle as shown. Make 20 (2½" x 6½").

2. Sew a 2½" fabric J square between two half-square triangles. Make 10 (2½" x 6½").

3. Arrange and sew three rows together as shown. Make 10 (6½" x 6½").

4. Sew a 2½" x 6½" fabric K rectangle to the top and bottom of a star. Make three (6½" x 10½").

5. Sew a 4½" x 6½" fabric K rectangle to a star. Make seven (6½" x 10½").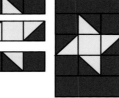

6. Arrange and sew nine star blocks and the two 2½" x 10½" rectangles in any order you like.

7. Sew a 4½" x 10½" rectangle to one side of the last star. (10½" x 10½").

8. Appliqué the moon in the space around the star, then sew the star/moon block to the end of the row (10½" x 68½").

9. Set the Star block row aside until all the blocks are completed.

Oh, Susannah!

Music was important for the family for teaching values as well as for entertainment. On long winter evenings, Pa played tunes on the fiddle and sang songs to the delight of the girls: songs that told stories, lively songs they could sing, and soft lullabies to put them to sleep at night.

Piecing

1. Sew the 2½" x WOF fabric H and L strips together along the long edge. Cut at 2½" intervals. Make 16 cuts (2½" x 4½").

2. Sew a 2½" H square on the diagonal to each 2½" x 4½" fabric B rectangle as shown. Make 16 (2½" x 4½"). See Flip Corners page 10.

3. Sew the strips and the rectangles together in pairs as shown. Make eight pairs (4½" x 8½").

4. Sew the pairs together. Make four (8½" x 8½").

5. Set the Oh, Susannah! blocks aside until all the blocks are completed.

Kitchen Wood Box

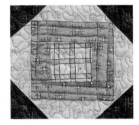

Every day Mary and Laura had to pick up wood chips from Pa's chopping block. They carried a pan full of chips into the house to kindle the morning fire. It was a chore they did not like, but I like the quilt block called Kitchen Wood Box.

Piecing

1. Sew 1½" x 2½" fabric C rectangles to opposite sides of each 2½" fabric I squares. Press away from the center as each piece is added. Sew a 1½" x 4½" fabric C rectangle to the top and bottom. Press. Make six (4½" x 4½").

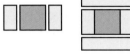

2. Sew a 1½" x 4½" fabric G rectangle to the sides and a 1½" x 6½" Fabric G rectangle to the top and bottom of the square as above. Make six (6½" x 6½").

3. Sew a 2½" fabric B square on the diagonal to opposite corners of each block as shown. Repeat with the remaining corners. See Flip Corners, page 10.

Note: You may wish to cut away the under half of the square leaving the corner of G as a piecing guide.

4. Set the Kitchen Wood Box blocks aside until all the blocks are completed.

Snail's Trail

This familiar block is also called Pig's Tail. When Pa butchered the pig, some was smoked and some salted, and some put to pickle in brine. The part the girls liked best was the pig's tail. After Pa skinned the tail, he put it on a stick. Laura and Mary took turns carefully turning it in the fire on the hearth. They ate every bit of meat and then gave the rest to their dog, Jack.

Piecing

1. Sew the 1½" x 14" fabric E and F strips together along the long edge. Cut at 1½" intervals. Make eight cuts (1½" x 2½").

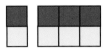

2. Sew two strips together alternating fabrics. Make four four-patches (2½" x 2½").

3. Cut all E and F squares in half diagonally.

4. Place the smallest fabric F triangle at the top of the four-patch with the fabric F square in the upper left. Center and sew in place. Repeat with the opposite side. Make four.

5. Sew the smallest fabric E triangle to each side of the four patch. Complete Round #1 by measuring from the center of the block 1⅝". Trim the block to measure 3¼". Make four.

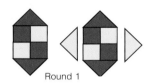
Round 1

6. Continue alternating fabrics in same manner. Trim from center. See the table below for proper sizes.

Note: The last round of color uses three F triangles and one E triangle. Check the diagram. Trim from the center to measure 8½" x 8½".

Round 2

Round 3

Round 4

	Trim from Center	Size of Round
Round #1	1⅝"	3¼"
Round #2	2¼"	4½"
Round #3	3"	6"
Round #4	4¼"	8½"

7. Arrange the blocks so that the large light triangles are toward the center or arrange the blocks any way you prefer! Measures 16½" x 16½".

8. Set the Snail's Trail block aside until all the blocks are completed.

Fence and Yard

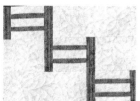

A fence was built around the garden to keep the deer and rabbits from eating Ma's garden. Pa cut down trees to let more sun reach the garden. At Christmas, the girls and their cousins climbed on the stumps. Then they fell face first into the snow, making snow pictures.

Piecing

1. Sew three 1½" D strips, and two 1" C strips, together along the long edge, beginning and ending with D strips. Cut at 4½" intervals. Make six (4½" x 4½").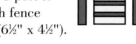

2. Sew a 1½" x 4½" C post to both sides of each fence block. Make six (6½" x 4½").

3. Sew a 5½" x 4½" D piece to both sides of two fence blocks (4½" x 16½").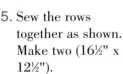

4. Sew a 10½" x 4½" D piece to one side of four fence units.

5. Sew the rows together as shown. Make two (16½" x 12½").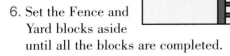

6. Set the Fence and Yard blocks aside until all the blocks are completed.

Log Cabin

This traditional block may use a red center to represent the chimney, the center of the home, or a yellow center to represent hospitality with a light in the window. Scraps are used to piece this block.

Piecing

1. For the log cabin, cut a center piece 2½" x 4½" from red to represent the chimney or tan to represent the light in the window.

2. Cut 1½" wide pairs of light scraps each: 4½", 6½", 8½", and 10½".

3. Cut 1½" wide pairs of dark scraps each: 4½", 6½", 8½", 10½", and 12½" long.

4. Sew a 4½" light strip to the top and bottom of the house center. Sew second pair of 4½" light strips to the ends.

5. Sew 6½" dark strips to the top and bottom of the block and then the sides of each block.

6. Continue to sew pairs in the same order to build the log cabin (12½" x 12½") ending with 12½" strips on the top and bottom.

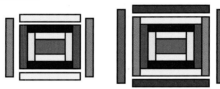
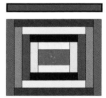

7. Set the Log Cabin block aside until all the blocks are completed.

Path through the Woods

There were deer trails through the woods. They knew the best way to travel, and Pa used these trails as he hunted, visited neighbors, or went to town.

Half-Square Triangles

1. Cut (16) 3" squares each from dark and light fabric scraps. Cut once diagonally.

2. Sew eight pairs of light and medium/dark triangles on the bias edge to make 16 half-square triangles. Trim to 2½". Press toward the dark.

3. Cut 3" squares each from six dark and six light scraps. Cut once diagonally.

4. Use the illustration to arrange the half-square triangles and remaining triangles in rows as shown. Match intersections carefully. Use a ruler to trim the bias edge of the triangles, leaving ¼" for seam allowance. Make four.

5. Cut 7½" squares of Fabric E and F in half diagonally. Center and sew one triangle to each side of triangle strips. Make four (8½" x 8½").

6. Arrange the squares so the paths of the triangles cross in the center. Make one (16½" x 16½").

7. Set aside the Path through the Woods block.

Piecing the Block Units

Tree Section

1. Cut four 6½" x 22½" fabric A borders.

2. Sew one to opposite sides of the tree. Press toward the tree.

3. Sew a Kitchen Wood Box block to each end of the two remaining borders.

4. Sew to opposite sides of the tree. Press toward the tree (22½" x 22½").

Unit A

1. Cut one fabric D 12½" square in half on the diagonal.

2. Center and sew the bias side of one triangle to the Snail's Trail block and one to the Path through the Woods block.

3. Cut one fabric D 17" square in half on the diagonal.

4. Sew short side of one triangle to the adjacent side of the Snail's Trail block and one to the adjacent side of the Path through the Woods block.

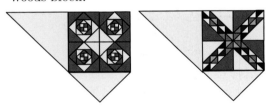

Note: Handle the bias edges very carefully.

5. Trim ¼" beyond the intersections of the blocks and triangles.

6. Sew the Snail's Trail unit to the upper right side of the tree section.

7. Sew the Path through the Woods unit to the lower left side of the tree section.

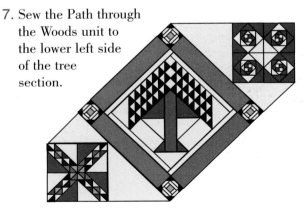

Unit B

1. Sew a 6½" x 10½" fabric C rectangle to a Wood Box block and to a Sister's Choice block as shown. Make two each.

2. Sew the blocks together.

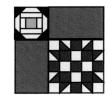

3. Cut four 9½" fabric C squares in half on the diagonal.

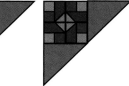

4. Sew a triangle to adjoining sides of each Oh, Susannah! block, matching to outer edges as shown. Make four.

5. Sew Oh, Susannah! blocks to adjoining sides of the Sister's Choice blocks. Make two.

Note: Handle bias edges very carefully while sewing and pressing.

6. Trim ¼" beyond the intersections of the blocks and triangles

7. Sew Oh, Susannah! units to the upper left and lower right of the tree section (48½" x 64½").

Unit C

Center section frame

1. Measure the quilt lengthwise through the center, and piece 2½" fabric I border strips this measurement. Sew to the sides of the quilt. Press toward the border.

2. Measure the quilt crosswise through the center, and piece 2½" border strips this measurement. Sew to the sides of the quilt. Press toward the border.

Log cabin and yard row

1. Sew the Bear Track, Fence, and Cabin blocks together as shown (12½" x 68½").

2. Sew the section to the bottom of the quilt.

Star Row

Sew the Star and Moon row across the top of the quilt (10½" x 68½").

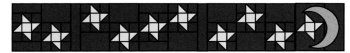

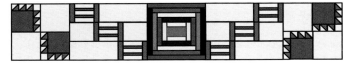

Inner Border

1. Measure the quilt lengthwise and cut two borders this measurement from 3½" strips of fabric B.

2. Sew to the sides of the quilt. Press toward the inner border.

3. Measure the quilt crosswise and cut two borders this measurement from 3½" strips of fabric B.

4. Sew to the top and bottom of the quilt. Press toward the inner border.

Outer Border

1. Measure the quilt lengthwise and crosswise then cut two borders of each measurement from 8½" strips of fabric A.

2. Sew the lengthwise pieces to the sides of the quilt.

3. Sew 8½" fabric B squares to each end of the remaining outer borders. Press toward the inner border.

4. Sew to the top and bottom of the quilt. Press toward the inner border (82½" x 88½").

Appliqué

1. The leaf appliqué is optional.

2. Use the leaf patterns on page 28 and follow the manufacturer's directions for iron-on adhesive.

3. Stitch in place.

Finishing

1. Sandwich, quilt, then bind with 2½" wide strips pieced to measure 400" inches.

2. Sign and date your quilt. Enjoy!

Bonnie Erickson's beautiful machine quilting is clearly seen on the reverse side of the quilt.

This stunning tree quilt was pieced by Julia Clark and Sandra Schafer as a gift to the author. Sandra's thread art illustrates the blocks of the larger quilt using colored thread.

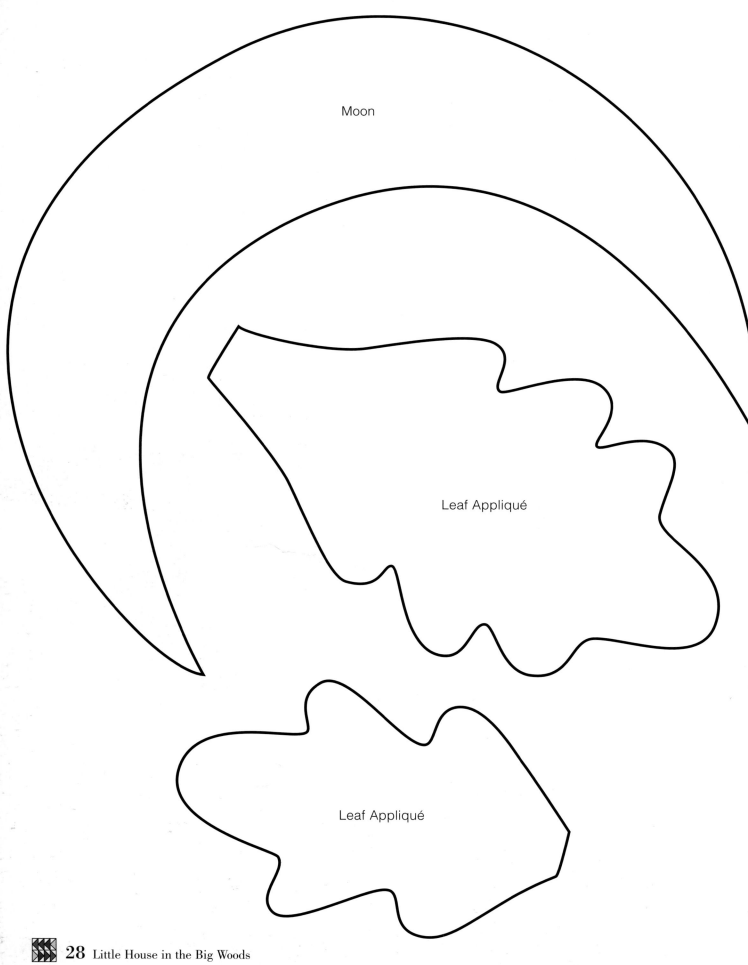

Moon

Leaf Appliqué

Leaf Appliqué

Little House on the Prairie

The Ingalls family travels by covered wagon from the woods of Wisconsin to the open prairie of Kansas. The trip is an exciting adventure for everyone but especially for the little girls. Laura is amazed at the vastness of the sky and the multitude of stars. They camp on their prairie homestead, and Laura and her sister, Mary, watch with anticipation as Pa builds their log cabin. The girls help with chores and enjoy exploring in the tall prairie grasses.

Vintage top from the author's collection
Machine quilted by Bonnie Erickson
80" x 96", 12" block

Glittering Stars

Laura gazed at the glittering stars from her bed in the wagon. She was sure Pa could reach one for her.

Materials

- 6¼ yd. white fabric for background, borders, and binding
- 20 fat quarters or 20 scraps at least 10" x 20" for blocks
- 6 yd. for backing
- 84" x 100" batting

Cutting Directions

	Number of Strips	Size to cut Strips WOF	Number of Pieces	Size of Pieces
Background	4	12½"	12	12½" x 12½"
	2	18"	4	18" x 18"
	3	4½"	20	4½" x 4½"
	1	9"	2	9" x 9"
	10	2½"	160	2½" x 2½"
Borders	9	6½"		
Binding	9	2½"		to equal 375"
Each block fabric		4½"	8	4½" x 4½"

Piecing

Make 20 blocks.
Review Double Flip Corners, page 10.

1. Sew a 2½" white square on the diagonal to opposite corners of a 4½" block square. Be sure the angle matches the illustration. Trim the inner triangle, press, flip, and press toward the triangle. Make four block squares with flip corners for each block.

2. Sew a 4½" block square to both sides of the square with flip corners. Make two. Press toward the block squares.

3. Sew a square with flip corners to both sides of the 4½" white square. Press toward the center square.

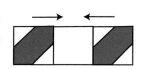

4. Arrange squares in rows and sew together, interlocking seams (12½" x 12½"). Make 20 star blocks.

Construction

1. Arrange and then sew the star blocks and 12½" white squares in diagonal rows.

2. Cut the 18" white squares diagonally twice for a total of 14 triangles.

 See Setting Triangles, page 9.

3. Sew a large triangle to the end of each row. Handle the bias edges of the triangles carefully.

Note: Line the large triangles up at the edge of the pieced blocks so they extend beyond the outside edge. Triangles will be trimmed in Step 7.

4. Cut the 9" white squares diagonally once for a total of four triangles.

5. Center a triangle on the end of each corner block.

Note: To find the center of the triangles, carefully fold them in half along the bias edge and finger press at the edge. Finger press the center of the block. Match the centers, and sew with the triangle on the bottom. Press toward the triangle.

6. Press the seams in all rows toward the white squares and triangles.

7. Sew the rows together. Trim the outer triangles ¼" beyond the edges of the pieced blocks.

Borders

Refer to page 12.

1. Measure and cut two borders the length of the quilt top. Sew them to the sides of the quilt. Press toward the border.

2. Measure and cut two borders the width of the quilt. Sew them to the top and bottom of the quilt. Press toward the border.

Finishing

Refer to page 12.

1. Sandwich, quilt, and then bind your quilt with 2½" wide binding strips pieced to measure 375".

2. Sign and date your quilt.

This purchased vintage quilt top is a colorful scrap quilt whose initial appeal was a block with which I was unfamiliar. When one fabric ran out, another was substituted in its place. Two of the blocks hardly show due to fading over the years. It was beautifully machine quilted by Bonnie Erickson.

Stitched by Bonnie Erickson
30" x 20"

Redwork Pillow Shams

Ma carefully opened the white pillow shams with red birds embroidered on them. As she placed them over the pillow, Laura was sure she had never seen anything so beautiful.

Materials

❖ 1 pair of purchased pillow cases
❖ Pearl cotton, red

Construction

1. Fold each pillow case in four quadrants to find center.

2. Gently press.

3. Trace two bird designs on each pillow case.

4. Embroider the designs with the stem stitch. (See page 10.)

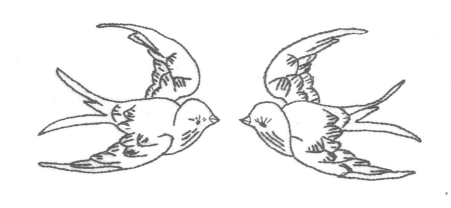

Pieced and appliquéd by Kathy Goral
22" x 19½"

Flowers for Ma

Laura and Mary enjoyed exploring the prairie and watching the small animals scurrying in the tall grasses.
They were fascinated by the gophers but decided to take Ma flowers rather than a gopher.

Materials

- ⅝ yd. for sashing, borders, and binding
- ⅓ yd. for window panes
- Fat quarter for stems
- 7" x 9" scrap for vase
- Scraps for flower shapes
- ¾ yd. for backing
- 24" x 24" batting
- Iron-on adhesive
- Several ¼" wide strips of lightweight cardboard 8" to 10" long

Cutting Directions

	Number of Strips	Size to cut Strips WOF	Number of Pieces	Size of Pieces
Sashing	1	4½"	1	4½" x 19¾"
	1	1¼"	1	1¼" x 17¼"
			2	1¼" x 8½"
Borders	1	4½"	1	4½" x 19¾"
			1	1½" x 19¾"
	1	1½"	2	1½" x 17¼"
Binding	3	2½"		
Window pane			4	8½" x 8½"
Stem		1¼" bias strips		to equal 65"
Flower pot			1	7" x 9"
Scraps for appliqué				

Piecing

1. Sew 1¼" x 8½" sashing strips between each pair of window panes. Press toward the sashes.

2. Sew a 1¼" x 17¼" sashing strip between the pairs of window panes. Press toward the sashes.

3. Sew a 1½" x 17¼" border strip to each side of the quilt. Press toward the border.

4. Sew a 1½" x 19¾" border to the top and 4½" x 19¾" border to the bottom of the quilt. Press toward the border.

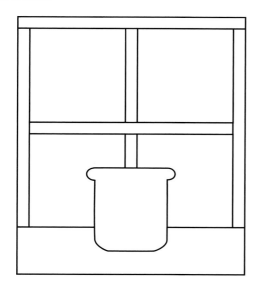

5. Prepare bias stems by folding the strips wrong sides together and sewing a ⅛" seam. Insert a ⅜" wide cardboard strip or pressing bar into the tube and twist the seam to the flat side of the cardboard. Press so the seam is on the back of the stem. Repeat until you have 65".

6. Pin the stems to the window panes in a pleasing manner, using the photo as a guide.

Appliqué

1. Prepare the flower shapes from designs found in the scrap fabrics. Cut graduated oblong pieces from the scraps for the flower pods. (Refer to the patterns on page 38.) Follow the manufacturer's directions for preparing the iron-on adhesive. Arrange and pin flower shapes in place.

2. Apply the iron-on adhesive to the wrong side of the flower pot (7" x 9"). On the backing paper, draw a line lengthwise through the center. Draw another paral- 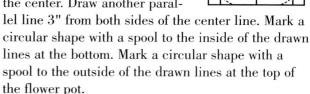 lel line 3" from both sides of the center line. Mark a circular shape with a spool to the inside of the drawn lines at the bottom. Mark a circular shape with a spool to the outside of the drawn lines at the top of the flower pot.

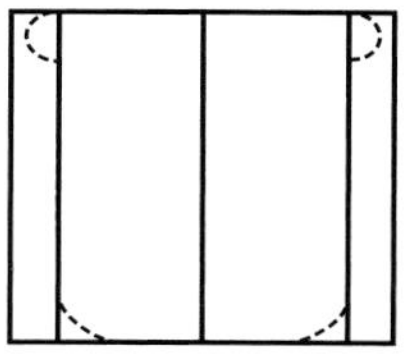

3. Cut on the lines and iron in place following the manufacturer's directions. You may wish to topstitch or satin stitch around the edges.

4. Embellish with buttons.

Finishing

Refer to page 12.

1. Sandwich, quilt, then bind your quilt with the 2½" wide binding pieced to measure 95".

2. Sign and date your quilt.

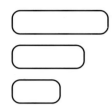

Farmer Boy

Almanzo Wilder lives on a dairy farm in upper New York State. Farmer Boy is a delightfully descriptive collection of stories of his life growing up on that farm. Cutting firewood, milking cows, planting crops, and caring for the horses are a few of his chores—some more pleasant than others!

Vintage quilt from the author's collection
56" x 64", 5" block

Churn Dash Quilt

When there was so much milk that they had to churn butter twice a week, Mother made Almanzo help with churning on rainy days. This was not his favorite chore.

Materials

- 4⅛ yd. white background fabric for blocks and binding
- 1⅔ yd. assorted navy/white prints
- 4 yd. for backing
- 60" x 68" batting

Cutting Directions

		Number of Strips	Size to cut Strips WOF	Number of Pieces	Size of Pieces
Background-Blocks		12	3"	144	3" x 3"
		15	1½"		
		8	5½"	56	5½" x 5½"
		2	8½"	8	8½" x 8½"
		1	4½"	2	4½" x 4½"
Binding		7	2½"		to equal 250"
Navy-Blocks		12	3"	144	3" x 3"
		12	1½"		

Piecing

Review Half-Square Triangles, page 9.

1. Make 288 half-square triangles using the 3" background and navy squares. (Trim to 2½" x 2½".)

2. Sew a 1½" background and a 1½" navy strip together along the long side. Press. Open and press toward navy strip. Make six sets of strips. Cut at 1½" intervals. Make 144.

3. Sew a triangle square to each side of a background and navy strip. Make 144 (2½" x 5½").

4. Sew three background and two navy strips together beginning and ending with background strips. Press toward navy strips. Make three sets of strips.

5. Cut at 1½" intervals. Make 72.

6. Arrange and sew rows together. Make 72 blocks (5½" x 5½").

Construction

1. Arrange and sew the pieced blocks and 5½" background blocks together in diagonal rows. Press toward the background.

2. Cut the 8½" background squares diagonally twice for a total of 30 triangles.

3. Arrange and sew the background triangles to the ends of each row. Handle the bias edges of the triangles carefully.

Note: Line the triangles up at the edge of the pieced blocks so they extend beyond the outside edge. Triangles will be trimmed in Step 7.

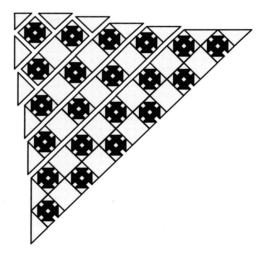

4. Press all rows toward the background blocks.

5. Cut the 4½" background squares diagonally once for a total of four triangles.

6. Center the triangles on the corner blocks. Press toward the triangle.

7. Sew the rows together, interlocking the seams. Trim the outer triangles ¼" beyond the edges of the pieced blocks.

Finishing

Refer to page 12.

1. Sandwich, quilt, and bind your quilt with the 2½" binding strips pieced to measure 250".

2. Sign and date your quilt.

This vintage Churn Dash quilt features a slightly different block variation.

Churn Dash is a vintage blue and white scrap quilt purchased in Iowa. The 5" blocks are set on point and hand stitched with tiny stitches. Though well used and worn in places it is one of my favorite vintage quilts.

Vintage blocks from the author's collection
Machine quilted by Bonnie Erickson
20" x 54", 10" block

Plaid Dash Table Runner

Almanzo may not have enjoyed churning butter, but he did enjoy eating it!

Materials

- ❖ (3) 11" x 11" dark scraps
- ❖ (3) 11" x 11" contrasting plaids
- ❖ Fat quarter for block frame
- ❖ ½ yd. for setting triangles and inner border
- ❖ ¾ yd. for outer border
- ❖ ⅓ yd. for binding
- ❖ ¾ yd. for backing
- ❖ 24" x 58" batting

Cutting Directions

	Number of Strips	Size to cut Strips WOF	Number of Pieces	Size of Pieces
Each Dark Scrap	1	2½"	1	2½" x 11"
	1	5"	2	5" x 5"
Each Light Scrap	1	2½"	1	2½" x 11"
	1	5"	2	5" x 5"
			1	2½" x 2½"
Frame	6	1½"	12	1½" x 18"
Setting Triangles	1	18"	1	18" x 18"
		1¾"	2	1¾" x 12"
			2	1¾" x 10½"
Outer Border	6	2¾"	2	2¾" x 35"
			2	2¾" x 17"
			2	2¾" x 16"
Binding	4	2½"	4	to equal 130"

Piecing

Review Half-Square Triangles, page 9.

1. Make four half-square triangles from the 5" light and dark squares for each block. (Trim to 4½" x 4½".)

2. Sew a pair of 2½" light and dark strips together along the long side. Press. Open and press toward dark strip. Make one set of strips for each block. Cut at 2½" intervals. Make four cuts for each block (2½" x 4½").

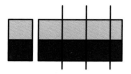

3. Sew a triangle square to each side of a background and dark strip. Make two for each block (4½" x 10½").

4. Arrange and sew strips together adding a 2½" light square at the center of the middle row.

5. Arrange and sew three rows together. Make three blocks (10½" x 10½").

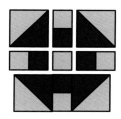
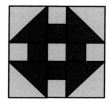

Block Frames

1. Measure across the center of each block and trim the 1½" frame pieces. Sew these to opposite sides of each block. Press toward the frame.

2. Measure across the center of each block in the opposite direction and trim the 1½" frame pieces. Sew them to the remaining sides of the blocks. Press toward the frame.

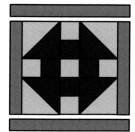

Setting Triangles

1. Cut the 18" square diagonally twice, making four triangles. Handle bias edges carefully.

2. Arrange blocks and large triangles in diagonal rows. Sew the triangles to the blocks, even with the edge at the center of the runner. Press toward each frame. Trimming will be done after borders are sewn on the ends.

3. Sew rows together.

Borders

1. Measure and sew a 1¾" x 10" strip to the block at each end of the runner.

2. Measure and sew a 1¾" x 12" strip to the adjacent side of each block.

3. Trim the sides of the runner, including the end borders, ¼" beyond the blocks on both sides.

4. Measure and sew 2¾" x 35" outer borders to each side of the runner. Press toward the outer border.

5. Measure and sew one 2¾" x 16" border to parallel ends of runner. Press after each seam and repeat with adjacent side (2¾" x 17").

6. Trim the ends of the runner even with the side borders.

Finishing

Refer to page 12.

1. Sandwich, quilt, and bind your quilt with the 2½" binding strips pieced to measure 130".

2. Sign and date your quilt.

The three vintage Churn Dash blocks were all different sizes and didn't have seam allowance at the ends of the triangles. I took the blocks apart and pressed very carefully. Even after careful assembly, the three blocks were not the same size, but they were square! I liked the plaids and was determined to use the blocks. I used a narrow border sewn around each block, then trimmed to one size. The table runner was completed with large triangles from fabrics designed at Plum Creek Patchwork. It is difficult to see the varying sizes of the borders now that the runner is finished, and I am very pleased with the finished product.

Pieced and hand quilted by the author
28" x 28", 10½" block

Bear Tracks in the Berry Patch

On warm summer days, the family would go berrying. Once, Almanzo ran into a black bear. The boy and the bear stood very still, watching one another, until the bear ran back into the woods.

Materials

- ½ yd. background fabric
- ½ yd. print for blocks
- ½ yd. for border
- ½ yd. for binding
- 1 yd. for backing
- 32" x 32" batting

Cutting Directions

	Number of Strips	Size to cut Strips WOF	Number of Pieces	Size of Pieces
Background	2	2½"	32	2½" x 2½"
	4	2"	2	2" x 11"
			1	2" x 23"
			16	2" x 5"
			16	2" x 2"
Print fabric	2	3½"	16	3½" x 3½"
			4	2" x 2"
	2	2½"	32	2½" x 2½"
Border	4	3½"		
Binding (bias)	3	2½"		to equal 125"

Piecing

Review Half-Square Triangles, page 9.

1. Make 64 half square triangles from 2½" background and print squares. Trim to 2" x 2".

2. Sew triangle squares together in pairs as illustrated. Make 16 pairs (2" x 3½").

3. Sew each pair to a 3½" print square. Make 16 (3½" x 5").

4. Sew the remaining triangle squares together in pairs as illustrated. Make 16 pairs. Sew a 2" background square to the left side of the triangles (2" x 5").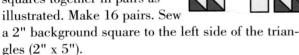

5. Sew the strip to the adjacent side of the square to complete one paw. Make 16 (5" x 5").

6. Sew a 2" x 5" background strip between two paws. Make eight (5" x 11").

7. Sew a 2" print square between two 2" x 5" background strips. Make four (2" x 11").

8. Arrange and sew paws and background strips together to make the block. Make four (11" x 11").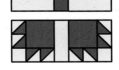

9. Arrange and sew the blocks and 2" x 11" background strips together. Make two (23" x 23").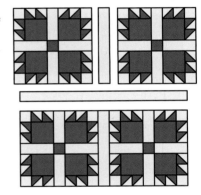

10. Sew a 2" x 23" background strip between the rows of blocks.

Borders

Refer to page 12.

1. Measure and cut lengthwise borders. Sew to the sides of the quilt. Press toward the borders.

2. Measure and cut crosswise borders. Sew to the top and bottom of the quilt. Press toward the borders.

Finishing

Refer to page 12.

1. Sandwich, quilt, then bind your quilt with 2½" wide binding strips pieced to measure 125".

2. Sign and date your quilt.

This quilt top was pieced and quilted before it was named. As I examined the background fabric I realized it had many kinds of berries scattered on it. The Bear Paws soon became "Bear Tracks in the Berry Patch." By chance, the name also fit perfectly with Almanzo's story.

Pieced by the author
Machine quilted by Bonnie Erickson
24" x 24"

Fourth of July Parade

It was breakfast time when Almanzo remembered the date. It was the Fourth of July, and the family was going to the parade in town.

Materials

- ⅓ yd. background fabric
- ½ yd. red print for star points and binding
- Fat quarter for star centers
- ¼ yd. for border
- 1 yd. for backing
- 28" x 28" batting

Cutting Directions

	Number of Strips	Size to cut Strips WOF	Number of Pieces	Size of Pieces
Background	1	5"	4	5" x 5"
	2	2¾"	4	2¾" x 9½"
			2	2¾" x 7¼"
			2	2¾" x 5"
			2	2¾" x 2¾"
Star centers (blue)	2	5"	5	5" x 5"
Star points (red)	2	2¾"	16	2¾" x 2¾"
Border	2	3½"		
Binding	3	2½"		to equal 110"

Piecing

Review Double Flip Corners, page 10.

1. Sew a 2¾" red square on the diagonal to opposite corners of a 5" background square. Trim the inner triangle, press, flip, and press again. Make four.

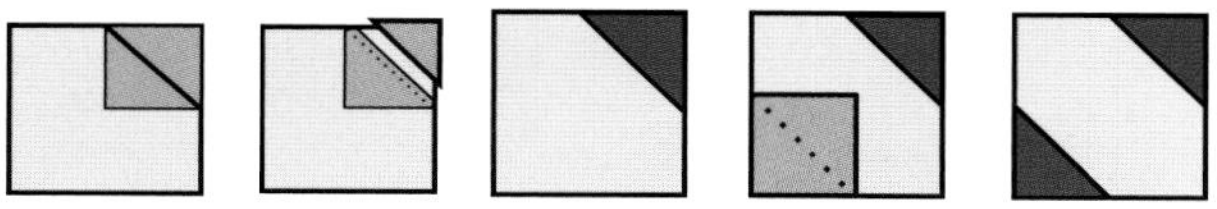

2. Arrange the flip corner blocks and the star centers in rows (5" x 14"). Press toward the star centers.

3. Sew the rows together (14" x 14").

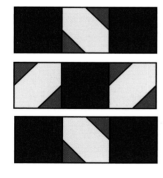 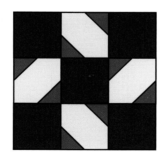

4. Sew one 2¾" red square on the diagonal of each background rectangle. Trim the inner triangle, press, flip, and press again. Make two 2¾" x 5", two 2¾" x 7¼", and four 2¾" x 9½".

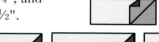

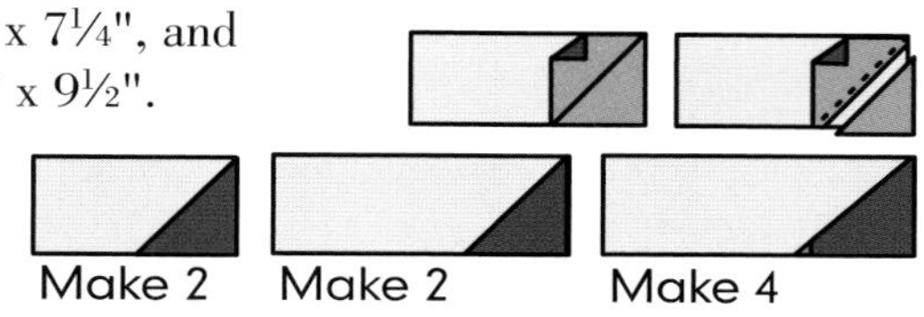

Make 2 Make 2 Make 4

5. Sew a 2¾" x 5" and a 2¾" x 9½" rectangle end-to-end. Make two (2¾" x 14"). Sew to the sides of the quilt. Press toward the red triangles.

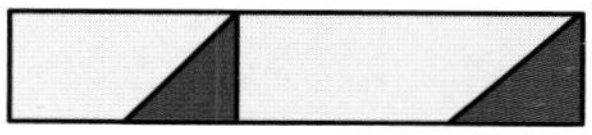

6. Sew a 2¾" x 7¼" and a 2¾" x 9½" rectangle end-to-end. Add a 2¾" background square to the end of the 9½" rectangle. Make two (18½" x 18½").

7. Attach the strips from Step 6 to the top and bottom of the quilt.

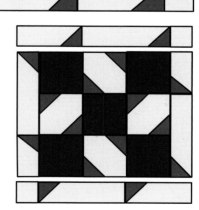

Borders

Refer to page 12.

1. Measure and cut two lengthwise borders. Sew to the sides of the quilt. Press toward the border.

2. Measure and cut two crosswise borders. Sew to the top and bottom of the quilt (24½" x 24½").

Finishing

Refer to page 12.

1. Sandwich, quilt, then bind your quilt with 2½" wide binding strips pieced to measure 110".

2. Sign and date your quilt.

Fussy cutting the circular design in the center blocks gives the illusion of motion, similar to pinwheels. Red, white, and blue always bring images of the Fourth of July. Changing the color could change the feeling of the "season."

On the Banks of Plum Creek

Pa moves his family to the banks of Plum Creek in Minnesota, where they live in a sod house. Later he builds a real log house. Life on the prairie is difficult for the settlers. Blinding winter blizzards are dangerous to man and beast. Summer heat, lack of rain, and grasshopper plagues make crops difficult to grow and nearly impossible to harvest. Hard work and making-do are necessary for survival. Storytelling, music, and stargazing offer the family pleasant diversions all year round.

Pieced and machine quilted by Kathy Goral
22" x 37"

Plum Creek in Summer

Pa drove to a flat place near Plum Creek and stopped the team. He looked around and declared that they had reached their destination.

Materials

- ❖ ⅓ yd. light for creek
- ❖ ⅓ yd. dark for season
- ❖ 2" x 18" scrap for block center
- ❖ ¼ yd. for inner border
- ❖ ⅜ yd. for outer border
- ❖ ¾ yd. for backing
- ❖ ⅓ yd. for binding
- ❖ 26" x 42" batting

Cutting Directions

	Number of Strips	Size to cut Strips WOF	Number of Pieces	Size of Pieces
Creek fabric	4	2"	1	2" x 17"
		2"	8	2" x 3½"
		2"	8	2" x 5"
		2"	8	2" x 6½"
Season fabric	5	2"	8	2" x 3½"
		2"	8	2" x 5"
		2"	8	2" x 6½"
		2"	8	2" x 8"
Center square	1	2"		2" x 17"
Inner Border	3	1½"		
Outer Border	3	3"		
Binding	3	2½"		to equal 130"

Piecing

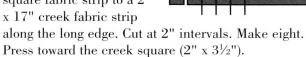

1. Sew a 2" x 17" center square fabric strip to a 2" x 17" creek fabric strip along the long edge. Cut at 2" intervals. Make eight. Press toward the creek square (2" x 3½").

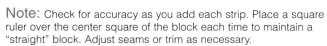

2. Sew a 2" x 3½" creek strip to the first step so that the last piece added (creek strip) is toward you. Make eight (3½" x 3½"). Press each additional piece toward the last piece added to the block.

Note: Check for accuracy as you add each strip. Place a square ruler over the center square of the block each time to maintain a "straight" block. Adjust seams or trim as necessary.

Continue adding pieces in the sequence indicated. Last piece sewn is always toward you as you add the next piece. Press toward the last piece added.

3. Add a 2" x 3½" season strip.

4. Add a 2" x 5" season strip (5" x 5").

5. Add a 2" x 5" creek strip.

6. Add a 2" x 6½" creek strip (6½" x 6½").

7. Add a 2" x 6½" season strip.

8. Add a 2" x 8" season strip. Make eight log cabin blocks (8" x 8").

9. Sew pairs of blocks with creek pieces together as shown. Make two of each (8" x 15½").

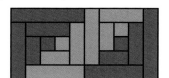

10. Arrange pairs of blocks creating a zigzag creek.

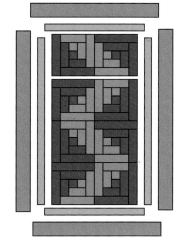

Borders
Refer to page 12.

1. Measure and cut lengthwise inner borders. Sew lengthwise borders to the sides of the quilt.

2. Measure and cut crosswise inner borders. Sew crosswise borders to the sides of the quilt.

3. Repeat sequence with outer borders.

Finishing
Refer to page 12.

1. Sandwich, quilt, and bind your quilt with 2½" wide binding to measure 130".

2. Sign and date your quilt.

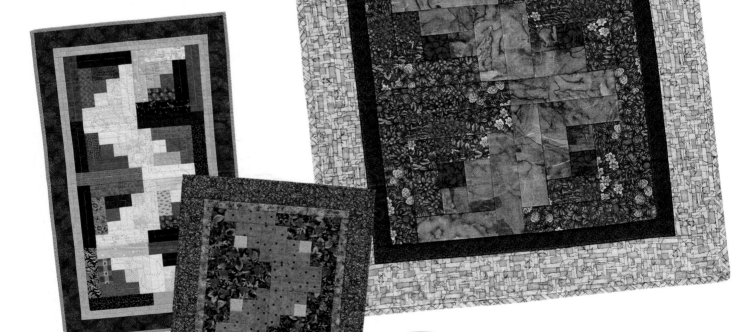

You can make a Plum Creek Table Runner for any season by changing the fabrics. We have shown additional examples for Plum Creek in Winter and Fall to help encourage your creativity.

Pieced by the author
Machine quilted by Bonnie Erickson
21" x 21"

Light in the Window

A dreadful wind was howling outside the cabin. Ma lit the lamp on the window sill to guide Pa home.

Materials

- ❖ ¼ yd. small red print
- ❖ ⅜ yd. tan background fabric
- ❖ ⅓ yd. large print for blocks and borders
- ❖ ⅓ yd. for binding
- ❖ ¾ yd. for backing
- ❖ 24" x 24" batting
- ❖ Pearl cotton, dark red

Cutting Directions

	Number of Strips	Size to cut Strips WOF	Number of Pieces	Size of Pieces
Small red print	3	1½"	2	1½" x 26"
			2	1½" x 15"
Tan background	3	1½"	1	1½" x 26"
			4	1½" x 15"
	1	4"	6	4" x 4"
	1	3½"	5	3½" x 3½"
Large print	1	4"	6	4" x 4"
Borders	1	3½"	4	3½" x 15½"
Binding	3	2½"		to equal 95"

Piecing

Review Half-Square Triangles, page 9.

1. Make 12 half-square triangles from 4" background and large print squares. Trim to 3½".

2. Sew a 1½" x 26" tan strip between two 1½" x 26" red strips. Press toward the red. Cross cut at 1½" intervals. Make 16 cuts.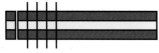

3. Sew a 1½" x 15" red strip between two 1½" x 15" tan strips. Press toward the red. Cross cut at 1½" intervals. Make eight cuts.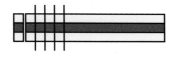

4. Alternate the strips as shown to make a nine-patch. Make eight blocks (3½" x 3½").

5. Sew a 1½" x 15" red strip between two 1½" x 15" tan strips. Press toward red. Cross cut at 3½" intervals. Make four cuts.

6. Arrange and sew nine-patches on each side of 3½" cut in rows as shown. Make two (3½" x 9½").

7. Arrange and sew a 3½" cut on each side of a 3½" background square as shown. Sew the three rows together.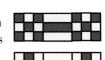

8. Sew one half-square triangle to each side of a 3½" background square. Make four. Sew one to each side of the center.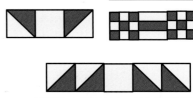

9. Sew one half-square triangle to each end of the remaining units from Step 8. Sew to the top and bottom of the center.

10. Trace the candle in the center block in the middle of the quilt. Hand stitch the design with the stem stitch. (See page 10.)

Borders

Refer to page 12.

1. Sew a border strip to each side of the quilt. Press toward the border.

2. Sew a four-patch at the end of each remaining border strip. Press toward the border.

Finishing

Refer to page 12.

1. Sandwich, quilt, and bind your quilt with 2½" wide binding strips to measure 95".

2. Sign and date your quilt.

Pieced by the author
Machine quilted by Bonnie Erickson
96" x 96"

Scrap Bag Quilt

Scraps from the clothes that Ma had made for her family were saved in her scrap bag. Ma made doll clothes for the girls and quilts for the family from her scraps.

Materials

- 3 yd. assorted dark prints for blocks
- 2 yd. assorted beige prints for blocks
- 5½ yd. blue print for sashing and border
- 1¼ yd. for binding
- 8½ yd. for backing
- 100" square of batting

Cutting Directions

	Number of Strips	Size to cut Strips WOF	Number of Pieces	Size of Pieces
Assorted dark prints	14*	2½" *		
	14*	5"	112	5" x 5", cut once diagonally
Assorted beige prints	14*	5"	112	4" x 4", cut once diagonally
Sashing	6	8½"	12	8½" x 16½"
Borders		16½" cut lengthwise	4	16½" x 66"
Binding (bias)	10	2½"		to equal 395"

*Cut more strips of shorter lengths for a scrappier quilt.

Piecing

1. Sew 2½" strips together along the long edge. Press toward the dark fabric. Cut at 2½" intervals. Make 112 cuts.

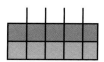 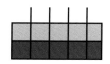

2. Sew two segments together to make a four-patch (4½" x 4½"). Make 56 four-patches.

See how to center pieces on page 9.

3. Center and sew a beige triangle on opposite sides of the four-patch. Press toward the triangle. Repeat with the remaining sides. Trim blocks ¼" beyond the four-patch corners to measure 6¼". Make 56.

4. Center and sew dark triangles in the same manner. Press toward the dark triangles. Trim the blocks to measure 8½" x 8½".

5. Sew the pieced blocks together in pairs. Press the seams in opposite directions. Sew pairs together. Make 13 blocks (16½" x 16½"). There will be four remaining four-patches.

6. Arrange large blocks, 8½" x 16½" sashing pieces, and four-patches in rows. Sew each row together. Press toward the sashing rectangles.

7. Sew the rows together. Press. Quilt center measures 64½" x 64½".

Borders

Refer to page 12.

1. Measure and cut lengthwise and crosswise borders. Sew the lengthwise borders to the sides of the quilt.

2. Sew a pieced block to each end of crosswise borders. Sew one to the top and one to the bottom of the quilt.

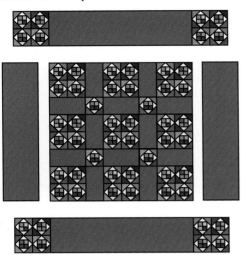

Finishing

Refer to page 12.

1. Sandwich, quilt, and bind your quilt with 2½" wide binding to measure 395".

2. Sign and date your quilt.

Use left-over blocks and fabrics to create a fun back for your quilt.

I had enough blocks sewn together to make an extra 16½" block which I centered on the back of the quilt. Great conversation piece!

If you have a collection of strips left from previous projects that are the size needed (or can be cut to the size needed) for the blocks, this is a good way to increase the variety of different fabrics in the quilt. I cut up so many pieces that there are enough waiting in a box to make another quilt!

By the Shores of Silver Lake

Pa heads west to unsettled territory in South Dakota after accepting a job working for the railroad. The family follows later. Mary's blindness, caused by scarlet fever while the family lived on Plum Creek, is the beginning of Laura's storytelling as she describes scenery and events to her sister. Ma and the girls travel by train from Walnut Grove to Tracy, a distance of 10 miles, where Pa meets them with the wagon. During the trip across the open prairie, Laura discovers bareback riding. As the railroad moves westward so do the Ingalls. The family spends the winter in the surveyor's house by the shores of Silver Lake.

Vintage top from the author's collection
Machine quilted by Bonnie Erickson
70" x 70", 8½" block

House that Pa Built

The house that Pa had built was but a speck on the vast prairie, but it gradually grew larger as the wagon came closer.

Materials

- ❖ 3 navy fat quarters for blocks
- ❖ 2 brown fat quarters for blocks
- ❖ ¾ yd. each 5 assorted light pink for blocks
- ❖ 2 yd. dark pink for alternate squares and setting triangles
- ❖ 1⅓ yd. for borders
- ❖ 4½ yd. print for backing
- ❖ 1¼ yd. coordinating print for binding
- ❖ 76" x 76" batting

Cutting Directions

	Number of Strips	Size to cut Strips WOF	Number of Pieces	Size of Pieces
From each navy			2	3½" x 18"
			10	3½" x 3½"
From each brown			2	3½" x 18"
			10	3½" x 3½"
From each light	1	3½"	2	3½" x 18"
	3	5½"	5	5½" x 5½"
	1	4"	10	4" x 4"
Setting triangles	2	14"	4	14" x 14"
Corner triangles			2	6½" x 6½"
Alternate blocks	5	9"	16	9" x 9"
Border	8	5½"		
Binding (bias)	8	2½"		to equal 290"

Piecing

The directions are for each navy/light and brown/light combination.

1. Sew one 3½" light strip between two 3½" dark strips. Press toward the dark. Cut at 3½" intervals five times.

2. Cut 5½" light squares diagonally twice.

3. Sew one triangle to opposite sides of a 3½" dark square. Make 10 of each combination.

4. Sew a strip with small triangles to the opposite sides of each dark/light/dark strip from Step 1.

5. Cut the 4" light squares diagonally once.

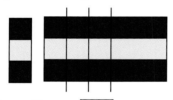
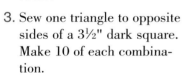
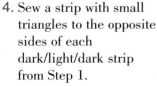
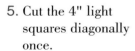

6. Center the triangle to the center of the each dark square. Sew the seam with the triangle on the bottom. Press toward the triangle.

7. Square the blocks to 9" by trimming ¼" beyond the seams.

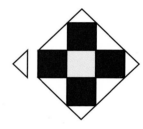

Construction

1. Arrange and sew the pieced blocks and 9" alternate squares in diagonal rows.

2. Cut the 14" squares diagonally twice for a total of 16 triangles.

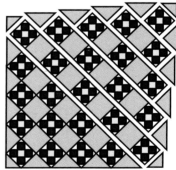

See Setting Triangles, page 9.

3. Sew a large triangle to the end of each row. Handle the bias edges of the triangles carefully.

Note: Line the large triangle up at the edge of the pieced blocks so they extend beyond the outside edge. Triangles will be trimmed in Step 7.

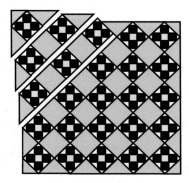

4. Cut the 6½" corner squares diagonally once for a total of four corner triangles.

5. Center a triangle on the end of each corner block.

6. Press the seams in all rows toward the alternate squares and border triangles.

7. Sew the rows together interlocking seams. Trim the outer triangles ¼" beyond the edges of the pieced blocks.

Borders

Refer to page 12.

1. Measure and cut two borders the length of the quilt top. Sew them to the sides of the quilt. Press toward the border.

2. Measure and cut two borders the width of the quilt. Sew them to the top and bottom of the quilt. Press toward the border.

Finishing

Refer to page 12.

1. Sandwich, quilt, then bind your quilt with 2½" wide binding strips pieced to measure 290".

2. Sign and date your quilt.

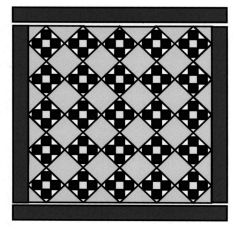

A wonderful "find" of a scrappy, bubblegum pink quilt top. Many of the pieces, no doubt cut from clothing, were worn and very fragile. It was quilted without pre-washing for fear of disaster.

Pieced by Cindy Thiese
Hand quilted by beginners in Bev Keltgen's class
54" x 72"

Mary's Nine-Patch

Mary could not understand why Laura wanted to stay out in the heat and watch the men move dirt for the railroad. She would rather stay in their clean house and make quilt blocks.

Materials

- 2⅛ yd. alternate plain blocks and end borders
- 23 navy/dark blue fabrics 8" x 8" scraps
- 2 red fabrics 8" x 8" scraps
- 25 white/tan fabrics 8" x 8" scraps
- 1¼ yd. for binding
- 4⅓ yd. for backing
- 60" x 76" batting

Cutting Directions

	Number of Strips	Size to cut Strips WOF	Number of Pieces	Size of Pieces
Alternate blocks	8	6½"	45	6½"
and borders	3	6½"		
Assorted navy prints	3 each fabric	2½"	66	2½" x 8"
Assorted light prints	3 each fabric	2½"	66	2½" x 8"
Reds	3 each fabric	2½"	6	2½" x 8"
Binding (bias)	7	2½"		to equal 110"

Note: Mary would have cut and sewed squares together one by one. If you wish to cut individual squares you will need 205 dark squares and 200 light squares each 2½" x 2½". We will use the rotary cutter to cut the strips, sew them together, and then cut them into segments. This method will create a strip of three squares without cutting each one. Our quilt will have two blocks made from the same fabrics, one with the same dark in the corners and one with the same light in the corners. If you wish a more scrappy quilt cut the 2½" x 8" strips from as many darks and lights as you wish and sew a different fabric in each row.

Piecing

1. Sew strips of blue/white/blue fabric together. Press toward the blue. Cut the strips at 2½" intervals to equal three cuts. Make a total of 69 cuts.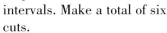

2. Sew strips of the same fabrics together white/blue/white. Press toward the blue. Cut the strips at 2½" intervals to equal three cuts. Make a total of 69 cuts.

3. Arrange and sew the strips together to make nine-patch blocks (6½" x 6½"). Make 23 nine-patches with blue corners and 23 nine-patches with white corners.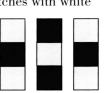

4. Sew strips of red/white/red fabric together. Press toward the red. Cut the strips at 2½" intervals. Make a total of six cuts.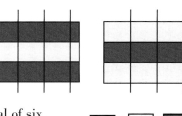

5. Sew strips of white/red/white fabric together. Press toward the red. Cut the strips at 2½" intervals. Make a total of six cuts.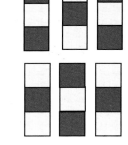

6. Arrange and sew the strips together to make nine-patch blocks (6½" x 6½"). Make two nine-patches with red corners and two with white corners.

Construction

1. Arrange and sew the five dark nine-patches and four plain squares in a row. Make five rows (6½" x 54½"). Press toward the plain squares.

2. Arrange and sew the five plain squares and four light nine-patches in a row. Make five rows (6½" x 54½"). Press toward the plain squares.

3. Sew the rows together, interlocking the seams.

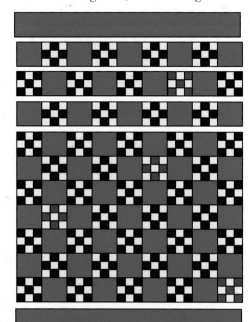

Borders

Refer to page 12.

1. Measure and cut two crosswise borders.

2. Sew the borders to the top and bottom of the quilt (6½" x 54½").

3. Press toward the border.

Finishing

Refer to page 12.

1. Sandwich, quilt, then bind your quilt with 2½" wide binding strips pieced to measure 110".

2. Sign and date your quilt.

When making this pattern, you will end up with five extra nine-patches. These can be used as a label on the back of the quilt, added as an embellishment to the edge of a pillowcase, or assembled with alternate blocks to create a pillow.

This quilt is a replica of the first quilt top I purchased many years ago. Each time I tried to use the top, I realized the fragile, not very square blocks it contained would have made finishing it very challenging. I decided to make a replica of the top instead. I didn't replace the missing side borders. The quilt was hand stitched by a group of beginning quilters with the encouragement of Bev Keltgen.

Vintage blocks from the author's collection
Machine quilted by Bonnie Erickson, 33" x 33"

Birds in the Air—Twilight

Ducks and geese landed on the lake in the approaching twilight. The wild ducks flew in straight lines; the wild geese flew in V's as they neared the water.

Materials

- Fat quarter or scraps of darks (navy)
- ¼ yd. or scraps for lights
- ¾ yd. for sashing and borders
- ⅓ yd. for binding
- 1 yd. for backing
- 36" x 36" batting

Cutting Directions

	Number of Strips	Size to cut Strips WOF	Number of Pieces	Size of Pieces
Darks	1	6⅞"	3	6⅞" x 6⅞"
	1	3"	9	3" x 3"
Lights	1	3"	9	3" x 3"
	1	2⅞"	9	2⅞" x 2⅞"
Sashing	1	6½"	2	9" x 6½"
			2	4¾" x 6½"
			3	3" x 6½"
	2	3"	2	3" x 23½"
Borders	4	3"		
Binding	4	2½"		to equal 145"

Piecing

Review Half-Square Triangles, page 9.

1. Make 18 half square triangles from nine 3" light and dark squares. Trim to 2½".

2. Cut the 2⅞" light squares in half diagonally.

3. Sew two half-square triangles together. Sew a small light triangle to each pair as shown. Make six.

4. Sew a small light triangle to the remaining half-square triangles.

5. Sew the two rows together. Sew a light triangle to the top.

6. Cut the 6⅞" dark squares diagonally once. Sew a large triangle to each pieced triangle section. Make six (6½" x 6½").

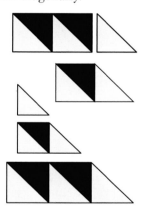

Construction

1. Arrange the blocks and the sashing in rows. Press toward the sashing.

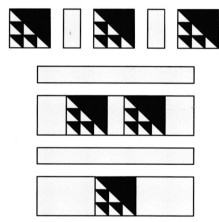

2. Sew the rows together.

Borders

Refer to page 12.

1. Measure and cut two lengthwise borders. Sew to the sides of the quilt. Press toward the border.

2. Measure and cut two crosswise borders. Sew to the top and bottom of the quilt (33½" x 33½").

Finishing

Refer to page 12.

1. Sandwich, quilt, then bind your quilt with 2½" wide binding strips pieced to measure 145".

2. Sign and date your quilt.

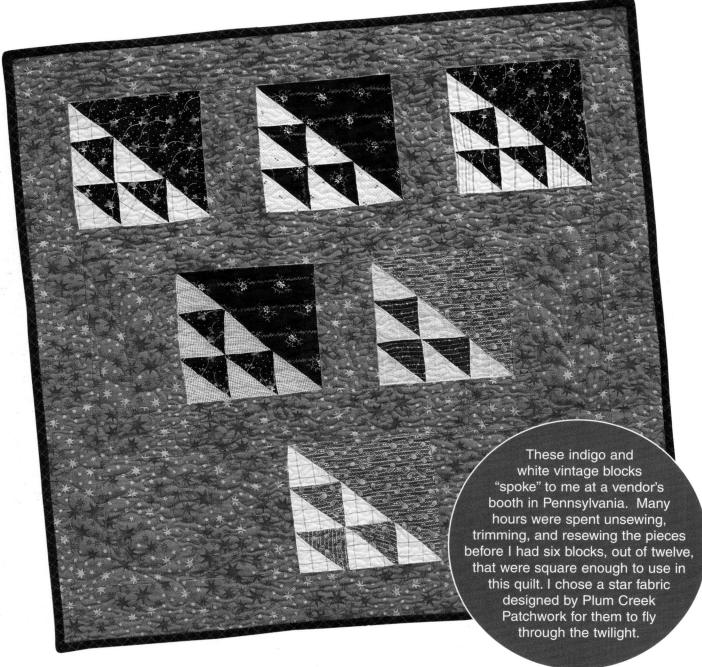

These indigo and white vintage blocks "spoke" to me at a vendor's booth in Pennsylvania. Many hours were spent unsewing, trimming, and resewing the pieces before I had six blocks, out of twelve, that were square enough to use in this quilt. I chose a star fabric designed by Plum Creek Patchwork for them to fly through the twilight.

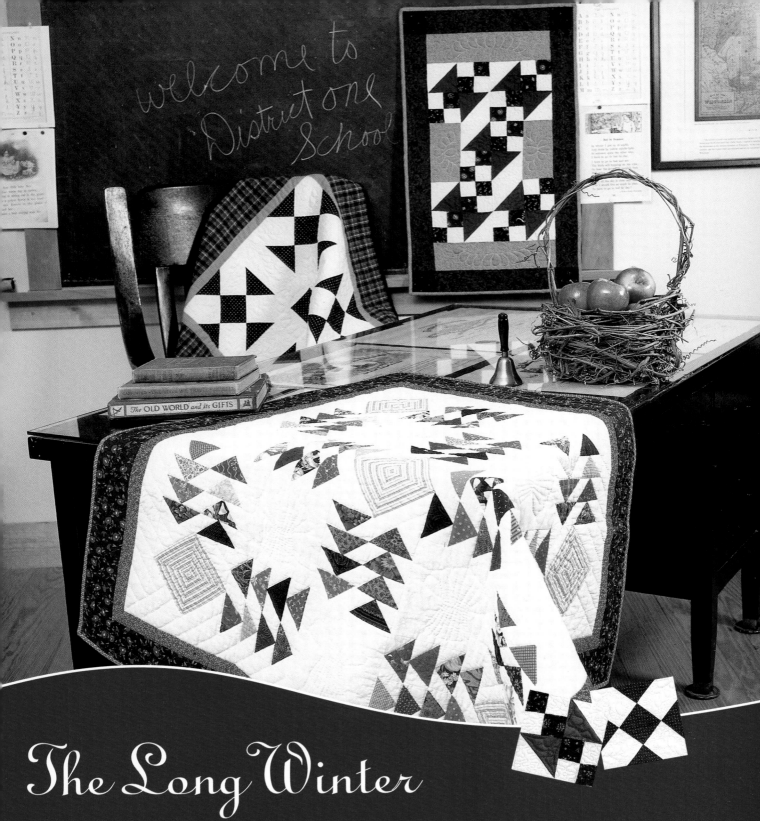

The Long Winter

The family moves into town for the winter, and it is lucky that they do. The village of De Smet, South Dakota, is snowed in by unrelenting blizzards beginning early in the fall. The food and fuel supply dwindle. Trains bringing winter supplies from the east are stopped by snow drifts across the tracks. Only the determination and courage of two young men keep the entire town from starving. They ride their horses, pulling sleds to a homestead some twenty miles from town where wheat is stored. The man there agrees to sell the wheat and helps load the sleds. They arrive back in town as another four-day blizzard strikes. The wheat supply lasts until the train finally arrives.

Vintage blocks from the author's collection
Machine quilted by Bonnie Erickson
30" x 30", 8½" block

Bachelor's Puzzle

The bachelor brothers, Royal and Almanzo Wilder, were in their warm back room frying pancakes when Charles Ingalls came calling.

Materials

- ❖ Fat quarter of navy
- ❖ ⅝ yd. white for background
- ❖ ⅛ yd. gold for inner border
- ❖ ⅔ yd. plaid for outer border
- ❖ 1 yd. print for backing
- ❖ ⅓ yd. coordinating print for binding
- ❖ 34" x 34" batting

Cutting Directions

	Number of Strips	Size to cut Strips WOF	Number of Pieces	Size of Pieces
Navy		3½"	5	3½" x 3½"
			4	5½" x 5½"
White	4	3½"	16	3½" x 5½"
			4	3½" x 9"
		2½"	16	2½" x 2½"
Gold	1	4½"	4	4½" x 4½"
	4	1½"		
Plaid Border	4	4½"		
Binding	4	2½"		to equal 130"

Piecing

1. Sew a 3½" navy square between two 3½" x 5½" white rectangles. Press toward the navy. Make four (3½" x 13½").

2. Cut 5½" navy squares diagonally twice. Handle bias edges carefully.

3. Sew a navy triangle to each side of a 3½" x 5½" white rectangle. Press toward the navy. Make 16.

4. Sew the rows together.

5. Position a square ruler so that adjacent sides are along the edges of the navy triangles and the horizontal seam line is straight. Trim along the edge of the ruler with a rotary cutter.

6. Turn the ruler and trim all four corners. Make four (9" x 9"). Handle bias corners carefully.

Construction

1. Sew a 3½" x 9" white sashing strip between each pair of blocks. Press toward the sashing. Make two (9" x 20½").

2. Sew a navy 3½" square between two white sashing strips. Arrange and sew the blocks and sashing. Sew the rows together (20½" x 20½").

Corner Border Blocks

Review Double Flip Corners, page 10.

1. Sew a 2½" white square on the diagonal to opposite corners of the gold square. Press, trim, flip, and press toward the triangle.

2. Repeat with remaining corners. Make four flip corner blocks for borders (4½" x 4½").

Borders

Refer to page 12.

1. Measure and cut two gold inner borders the length of the quilt top. Sew them to the sides of the quilt. Press toward the border.

2. Measure and cut two gold inner borders the width of the quilt. Sew them to the top and bottom of the quilt. Press toward the border.

3. Measure and cut two plaid outer borders the length and two the width of the quilt top. Sew the borders to the sides of the quilt. Press toward the first border.

4. Sew a pieced gold and white block to the end of each remaining plaid border. Press toward the block. Sew to the top and bottom of the quilt (30½" x 30½").

Finishing

Refer to page 12.

1. Sandwich, quilt, then bind your quilt with 2½" wide binding strips pieced to measure 130".

2. Sign and date your quilt.

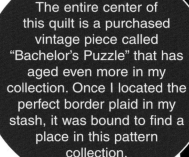

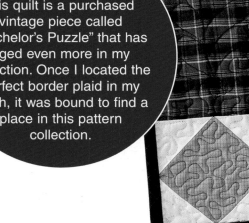

The entire center of this quilt is a purchased vintage piece called "Bachelor's Puzzle" that has aged even more in my collection. Once I located the perfect border plaid in my stash, it was bound to find a place in this pattern collection.

Pieced and hand quilted by the author
38" x 38", 6" x 6" block

Wild Goose Chase

Pa reported the talk in town about a settler to the south having a store of wheat on his property. Ma hoped that Pa wasn't going on a wild goose chase in search of that wheat.

Materials

- 1½ yd. off white for background and first border
- Scraps to measure ⅝ yd. for geese
- Fat quarter stripe for pieced squares
- ¼ yd. red print for border #2
- ½ yd. floral for border #3
- ½ yd. coordinating plaid for binding
- 1¼ yd. print for backing
- 42" x 42" batting

Cutting Directions

	Number of Strips	Size to cut Strips WOF	Number of Pieces	Size of Pieces
Background	2	6½"	8	6½" x 6½"
	10	2"	192	2" x 2"
	2	4"	20	4" x 4"
First border	4	2"		
Geese	9 (or scraps)	2"	96	2" x 3½"
Stripe	5	3"		template
Border #2	4	1½"		
Border #3	4	3½"		
Backing				42" x 42"
Binding (bias)	4	2½"		to equal 170"

Piecing

Review Flip Corners, page 10.

1. Sew a 2" background square on the diagonal to each 2" x 3½" goose rectangle. Trim the inner triangle, press, flip, and press. Repeat with a second square on the other end of each rectangle. Make 96 geese rectangles (2" x 3½").

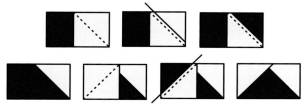

2. Sew four geese in formation. Make two lines for each block (3½" x 6½"). Sew two geese rows together so they are flying in opposite directions. Make 12 blocks (6½" x 6½").

3. Make a triangle template for the stripe fabric by cutting a 4" cardboard square once on the diagonal. Tape the triangle to the corner of a small square ruler so that the edges of the triangle are at the edge of the ruler.

4. Place a ruler with the long edge of the template at the bottom of the stripe fabric (stripe should run parallel to the long edge of the triangle). Cut on both sides of the template. Turn the ruler to the opposite side of the stripe and make another cut. Continue to the end of the strip. Repeat until you have made 20 stripe triangles.

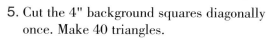

5. Cut the 4" background squares diagonally once. Make 40 triangles.

6. Place a stripe triangle and a background triangle with right sides together. Sew the triangles together along the bias edge with a ¼" seam. Make 40 triangle squares. Press toward the stripe fabric and trim to 3½".

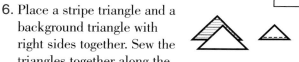

7. Arrange and sew the triangle squares in pairs. Sew pairs together so that stripes create a square on point when four are sewn together. Make five blocks (6½" x 6½").

8. Arrange and sew the pieced blocks, striped blocks, and background squares together in rows. Sew the rows together. Press toward the background squares and the stripe blocks.

Borders

Refer to page 12.

1. Measure and cut two inner borders the length of the quilt top. Sew them to the sides of the quilt. Press toward the border.

2. Measure and cut two inner borders the width of the quilt. Sew them to the top and bottom of the quilt. Press toward the border.

3. Measure and cut two outer borders the length of the quilt top. Sew them to the sides of the quilt. Press toward the first border.

4. Measure and cut two outer borders the width of the quilt. Sew them to the top and bottom of the quilt. Press toward the first border (38½" x 38½").

Finishing

Refer to page 12.

1. Sandwich, quilt, then bind your quilt with 2½" wide binding strips pieced to measure 170".

2. Sign and date your quilt.

The Mini Wild Goose Chase is 16" square. It is made from 4" blocks with 1" and 2" borders. Use scraps for the blocks.

Geese: (32) 1½" x 2½" rectangles with 1½" squares for the flip corners.

Striped squares: Eight 2½" finished half-square triangles.

Alternate blocks: (3) 4½" squares

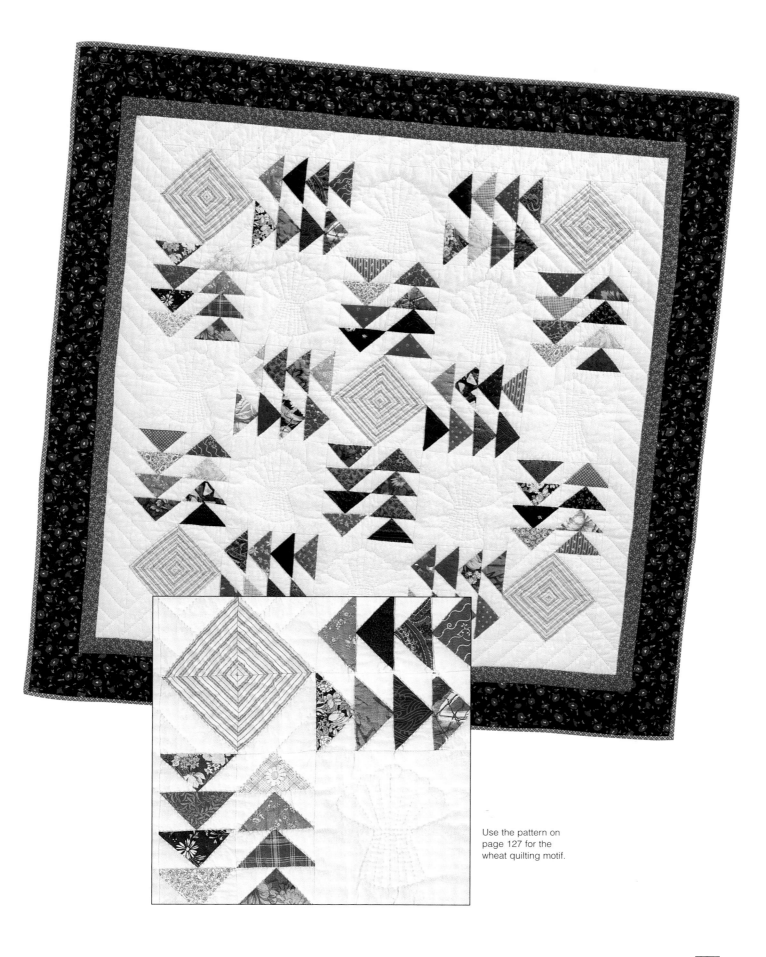

Use the pattern on
page 127 for the
wheat quilting motif.

Vintage blocks from the author's collection
Machine quilted by Bonnie Erickson
20" x 33", 7" block

Railroad Crossing

The food supply was dwindling, and the town was faced with imminent starvation when the long awaited train whistle was heard in the distance. The train had finally arrived from the East, bringing life-saving supplies.

Materials

- ❖ Scraps of dark green for blocks
- ❖ Fat quarter white for blocks
- ❖ Scraps of navy print for blocks and border corners
- ❖ ½ yd. of navy check for sashing and binding
- ❖ ¼ yd. turquoise for outer border
- ❖ 1 yd. for backing
- ❖ 24" x 36" batting

Cutting Directions

	Number of Strips	Size to cut Strips WOF	Number of Pieces	Size of Pieces
Dark green - blocks			5	4½" x 4½"
White blocks	2	4½" x 22"	5	4½" x 4½"
	3	2¼" x 22"	5	2¼" x 10"
Navy print - blocks			5	2¼" x 10"
Border corners			4	3½" x 3½"
Navy check- sashing	1	3½"	2	3½" x 7½"
	1	3½"	2	3½" x 14½"
Outer borders	2	3½"		
Binding (bias)		2½"		to equal 125"

Piecing

Review Half-Square Triangles, page 9.

1. Make 10 half-square triangles from the 4½" green and white squares. Trim to 4".

2. Sew 2¼" x 10" strips of navy and white fabric together. Press toward the navy. Cut strips at 2¼" intervals (2¼" x 4"). Make four cuts of each fabric combination for a total of 20 cuts.

3. Arrange and sew cuts together to make two four-patch blocks of each combination (4" x 4").

4. Arrange and sew triangle squares and four-patches together in rows.

5. Sew rows together to complete each block (7½" x 7½").

6. Arrange blocks and sashing in rows (7½" x 14½"). Sew the rows together (14½" x 27½").

Borders

Refer to page 12.

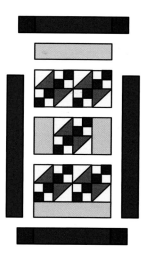

1. Measure and cut two crosswise borders and two lengthwise borders. Set aside.

2. Sew two lengthwise borders to the sides of the quilt. Press toward the border.

3. Sew one 3½" navy square to each end of crosswise borders. Press toward block. Sew to the sides of the quilt (20½" x 33½").

Finishing

Refer to page 12.

1. Sandwich, quilt, then bind your quilt with 2½" wide binding strips pieced to measure 125".

2. Sign and date your quilt.

Purchased vintage blocks from my collection were used is this table runner. The blocks were of various sizes, offering a challenge for piecing the top. Using fabric from my stash to complete a project always makes me glad I saved all those yards and yards!

Little Town on the Prairie

The family moves back to the claim shanty for the summer. Laura is happy to be out in the wide open spaces. She gives up the freedom when offered a sewing job in De Smet to provide money for Mary's college fund. Mary leaves home to attend the School for the Blind, and Laura and Carrie go to school in town. There is more activity in town, but Laura yearns for the prairie. Ma and Pa travel by train to visit Mary at college.

Hand-pieced vintage top, hand quilted by the ladies of Walnut Grove
63½" x 72½", 6" block

Four in a Nine-Patch

It was not always easy for a farmer to make his living on the prairie. Pa spent long days working alone in the fields without any machinery. Mother Nature sometimes worked against him, too. He had to plant four corn kernels in each hill: one for the blackbird, one for the crow, and two to grow.

Materials

- ❖ 11 dark/ medium fat quarters
- ❖ 55 light scraps 1½" x 18"
- ❖ 2¼ yd. for alternate squares and borders
- ❖ 1¼ yd. for binding
- ❖ 4½ yd. for backing
- ❖ 68" x 76" batting

Cutting Directions

	Number of Strips	Size to cut Strips WOF	Number of Pieces	Size of Pieces
From each dark fat quarter	5	1½"	5	1½" x 18"
	5	2½"	216	2½" x 2½"
From light scraps	55	1½" x 18"		
Alternate squares	9	6½"	54	6½" x 6½"
Border	4	5"		
Binding (bias)	8	2½"		to equal 290"

Piecing

1. Sew 1½" x 18" dark and light strips together lengthwise. Press toward dark then cut at 1½" intervals. Make 10 cuts for each block for a total of 550. Mix up the strips for more variety.

2. Sew pairs of cuts together to make five four-patches for each block.

3. Arrange and sew four-patches and 2½" squares in rows.

4. Sew rows together to make the nine-patch.

Construction

1. Arrange the nine-patches and the alternate blocks in rows. Press toward the alternate blocks.

2. Sew together, interlocking seams.

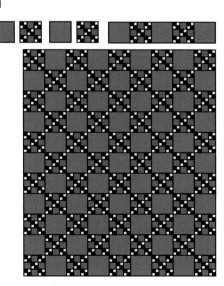

Borders

Refer to page 12.

Measure and cut two borders the length of the quilt top. Sew them to the sides of the quilt. Press toward the border.

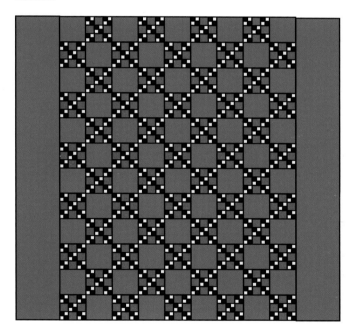

Finishing

Refer to page 12.

1. Sandwich, quilt, then bind your quilt with 2½" wide binding strips pieced to measure 290".

2. Sign and date your quilt.

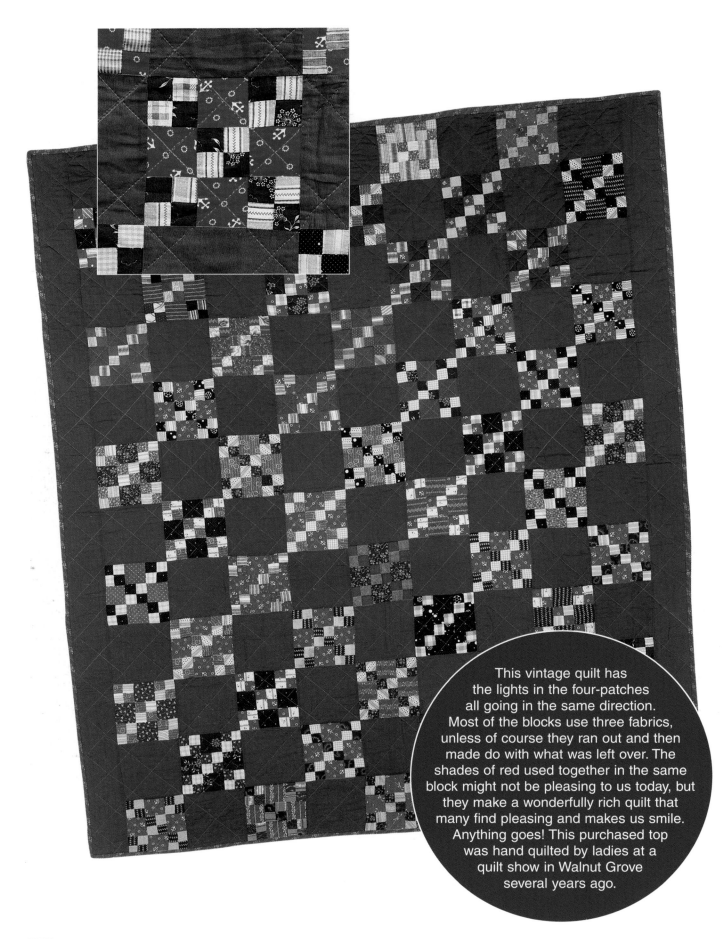

This vintage quilt has the lights in the four-patches all going in the same direction. Most of the blocks use three fabrics, unless of course they ran out and then made do with what was left over. The shades of red used together in the same block might not be pleasing to us today, but they make a wonderfully rich quilt that many find pleasing and makes us smile. Anything goes! This purchased top was hand quilted by ladies at a quilt show in Walnut Grove several years ago.

Pieced and appliquéd by Kathy Goral
26" x 26", 9" block

Prairie Queen

In spite of her blindness, Mary so enjoyed her walks across the ever-changing prairie. She felt like a queen with Laura describing the prairie flowers and the racing clouds.

Materials

- ❖ 1 yd. white for background and borders
- ❖ ½ yd. blue print for blocks and binding
- ❖ ⅓ yd. tan print for vine
- ❖ Scraps for appliqué
- ❖ ⅞ yd. for backing
- ❖ 30" x 30" batting
- ❖ Iron-on adhesive
- ❖ ¼" wide strip of lightweight cardboard

Cutting Directions

	Number of Strips	Size to cut Strips WOF	Number of Pieces	Size of Pieces
White	1	4"	8	4" x 4"
	2	2"		
	1	3½"	4	3½" x 3½"
	1	3"	18	3" x 3"
Borders	4	4½"		
Blue print	1	4"	8	4" x 4"
	2	2"		
Binding	3	2½"		to equal 120"

Piecing

Review Half-Square Triangles, page 9.

1. Make 16 half-square triangles from white and blue 4" squares. Trim to 3½".

2. Sew 2" strips of white and blue together. Press toward blue. Cut at 2" intervals. Make 32 cuts.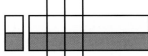

3. Sew the cuts together to make four-patches. Make 16 (3½" x 3½").

4. Arrange and sew the triangles squares, four patches and 3½" white squares in rows. Sew the rows together. Make four blocks (9½" x 9½").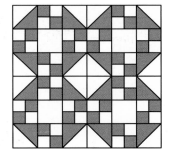

5. Sew the blocks together in pairs. Sew the pairs together (18½" x 18½").

Borders

Refer to page 12.

1. Measure and cut two lengthwise borders. Sew to the sides of the quilt. Press toward the border.

2. Measure and cut two crosswise borders. Sew to the top and bottom of the quilt (26½" x 26½").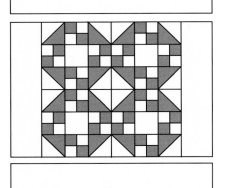

Appliqué

1. Cut 1¼" bias strips from vine fabric. Piece if necessary to make two strips at least 25" long. Press wrong sides together then stitch a ⅛" seam along edge. Slip a strip of ¼" wide cardboard inside the tube and turn the seam to one side of the cardboard. Press.

2. Arrange the vine in a pleasing manner. Sew in place by hand or machine.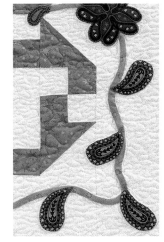

3. Locate various size motifs on fabric scraps suitable for appliqué. Follow the manufacturer's directions to prepare fabric for iron-on adhesive.

4. Apply to the quilt top, and then stitch in place.

Finishing

Refer to page 12.

1. Sandwich, quilt, then bind your quilt with 2½" wide binding strips pieced to measure 120".

2. Sign and date your quilt.

Prairie Queen, an old block, is given a fresh look in this wall quilt with the addition of appliquéd flowers and vines. The flowers and leaves are simply motifs found within your chosen fabric. This easy embellishment technique can be used to enliven any of your pieced projects.

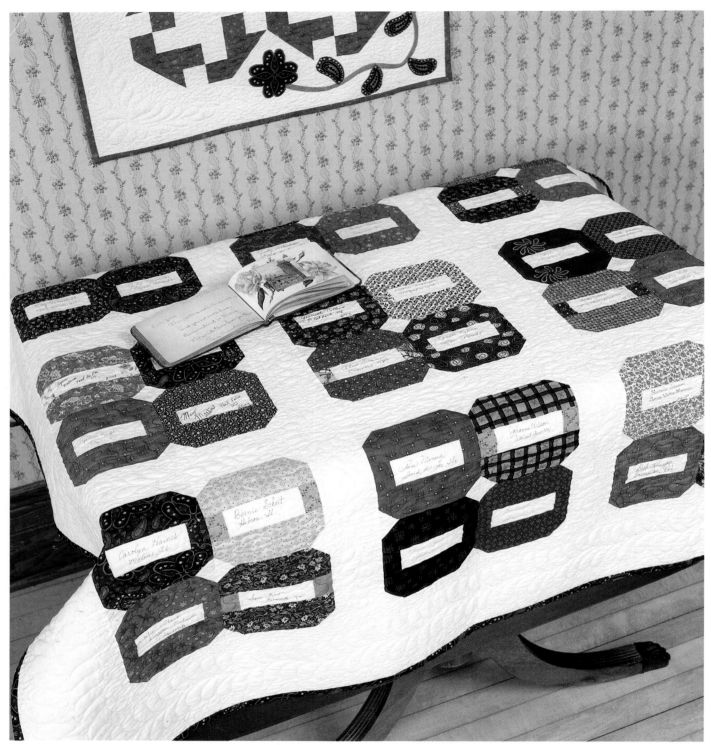

Pieced by Karla Schultz
Machine quilted by Bonnie Erickson
60" x 60", 6" block

Album Quilt

When Pa and Ma went to Iowa to visit Mary at the school for the blind, they brought back gifts for the other girls. Laura's gift was a small autograph book with a red cover. Now she could collect messages written by her school friends.

Materials

- ❖ 8" x 8" print scrap for each block (36)
- ❖ 2½ yd. muslin
- ❖ ½ yd. for binding
- ❖ 3⅔ yd. for backing
- ❖ 64" x 64" batting

Cutting Directions

	Number of Strips	Size to cut Strips WOF	Number of Pieces	Size of Pieces
Print Scraps for each block	2	2¾"	2	2¾" x 6½"
	1	1½"	2	1½" x 2"
Muslin - blocks	5	2"	36	2" x 4½"
	6	1½"	144	1½" x 1½"
Muslin - sashing	5	3½"	6	3½" x 12½"
			2	3½" x 48½"
Muslin - borders	7	6½"		
Binding	7	2½"		to equal 250"

Piecing

1. Sew a 1½" x 2" scrap to each end of a 2" x 4½" muslin rectangle. Press toward the scraps.

2. Sew a 2¾" x 6½" scrap rectangle to the top and the bottom the muslin rectangle.

3. Sew a 1½" muslin square on the diagonal to each of the four corners of the block. Trim the inner triangle, then press, flip, and press again. Make four.

4. Sew the blocks together in pairs. Sew the pairs together to make a 12½" block. Make nine blocks.

Construction

1. Arrange and sew the blocks and 3½" x 12½" sashing strips together in rows. Make three rows (12½" x 48½").

2. Piece, and then sew sashing strips between the rows of blocks.

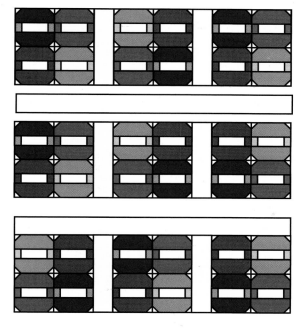

Borders

Refer to page 12.

1. Measure and cut two lengthwise borders. Sew to the sides of the quilt. Press toward the border.

2. Measure and cut two crosswise borders. Sew to the top and bottom of the quilt (60½" x 60½"). Press toward the borders.

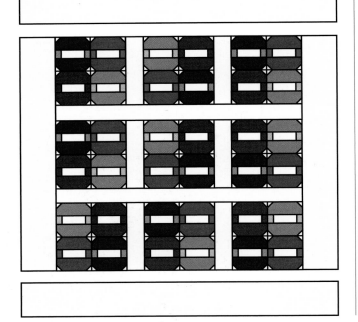

Finishing

Refer to page 12.

1. Sandwich, quilt, then bind your quilt with 2½" wide binding strips pieced to measure 250".

2. Sign and date your quilt.

Autograph albums often included verses. Here are a few examples from Laura's era:

❖ If scribbling in albums
Remembrance insures,
With the greatest of pleasures
I'll scribble in yours.

Your friend,
— Sadie Holbreck
  Sept. 17, 1899

❖ Dear Sister,
Long may you live
Happy may you be
Loved by all,
But best by me.

Your sister,
— Manie
  July 28, 1899

❖ Dear Jane,
May happiness be thy lot,
And peace thy steps attend;
Accept this tribute of respect,
From one who is thy friend.
— Lizzie Fox
  Mar. 5, 1900

❖ Friend Jane,
If you love me as I love you,
no knife can cut
our love in two.
— Minnie Brower
  Aug. 19, 1900

❖ Dear Janie,
When rocks and hills divide
us, and you no more I see,
Remember it was a friend
sincere, who wrote these lines
for thee.

Your friend and schoolmate
— Ervin A. Rinebolt
  Sept. 7, 1901

❖ Sister Jane,
I live for those who love me
and whose hearts are kind
and true, for the heaven that
smiles above me and awakes
my spirit too.

Your brother,
— Howard Black
  Jan. 12, 1904

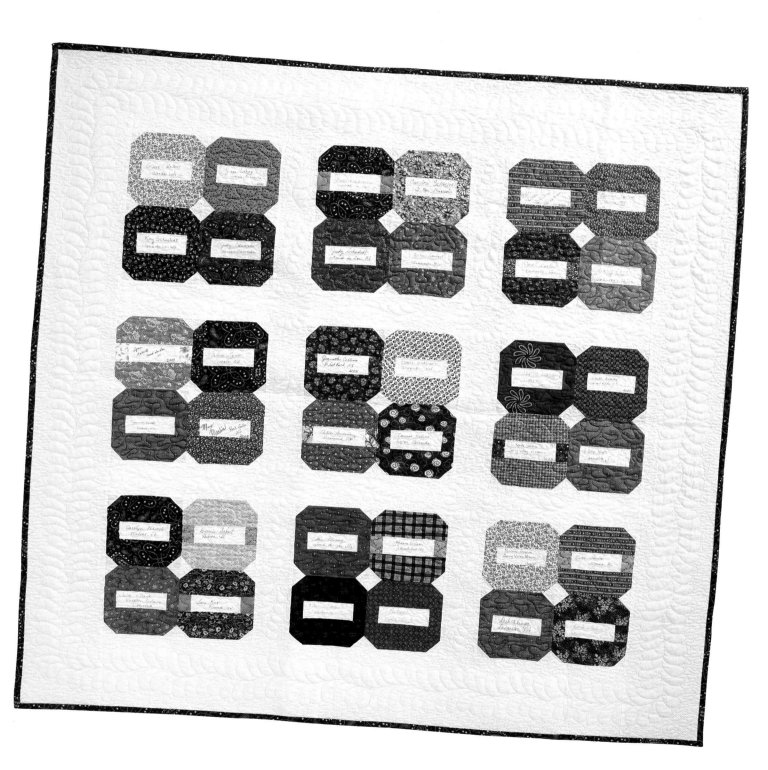

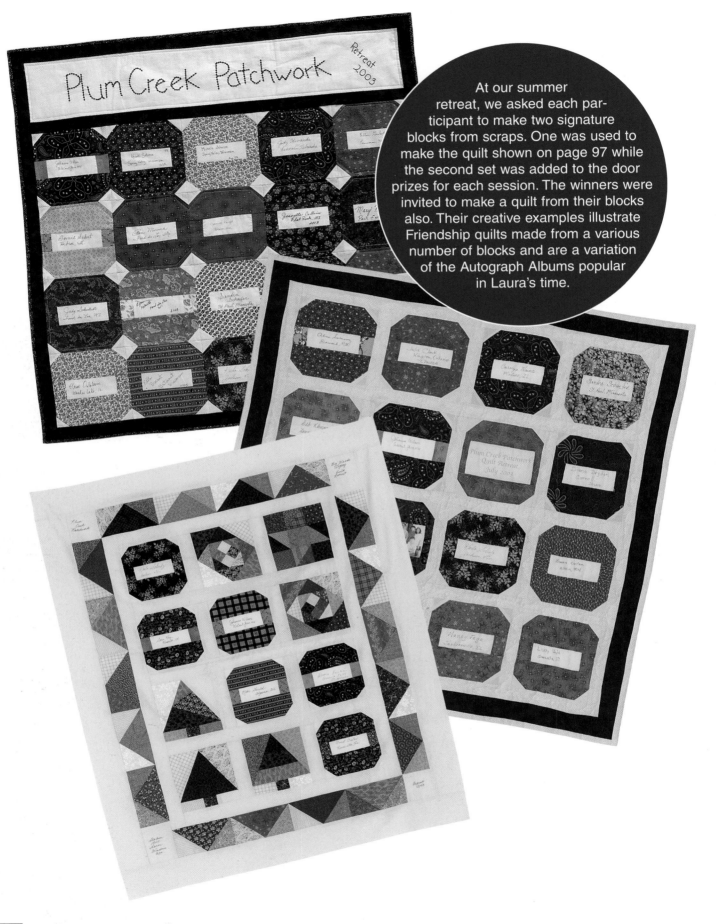

At our summer retreat, we asked each participant to make two signature blocks from scraps. One was used to make the quilt shown on page 97 while the second set was added to the door prizes for each session. The winners were invited to make a quilt from their blocks also. Their creative examples illustrate Friendship quilts made from a various number of blocks and are a variation of the Autograph Albums popular in Laura's time.

These Happy Golden Years

Laura's days as a student quickly end when she is hired to teach in a country school twelve miles from town where many of the students are bigger than she is. She overcomes the hardships of the new job as she continues to earn money for Mary's college expenses. Each Friday, Pa or Almanzo arrive to bring her home for the weekend. The carefree years while Almanzo is courting reveal Laura's steadfast love of family, her hard work, and her enthusiasm for driving horses—the faster the better!

Pieced by the author
Machine quilted by Bonnie Erickson
48" x 54", 10" block

Sister's Choice Wall Quilt

All sisters have to make choices. When Mary questioned Laura's intention to marry "that Wilder boy," Laura explained that he was her Almanzo, and it was time to begin a new life with him. Mary realized that Laura was growing up and moving on, just as she had done when she went away to college.

Materials

- ⅔ yd. red
- ⅝ yd. yellow/red check
- ¼ yd. red/yellow plaid
- 1⅓ yd. red check for sashing and binding
- ¾ yd. yellow/white check
- ⅝ yd. large white/red/yellow plaid
- ¼ yd. stripe
- 1 yd. large floral
- 3⅓ yd. for backing
- 54" x 60" batting

Cutting Directions

	Number of Strips	Size to cut Strips WOF	Number of Pieces	Size of Pieces
Red	3	3"	32	3" x 3"
	2	2½"	28	2½" x 2½"
	2	2½"		
Yellow/red check	2	3"	24	3" x 3"
	2	2½"	25	2½" x 2½"
	2	2½"		
Red/yellow plaid	1	3"	4	3" x 3"
	1	2½"	5	2½" x 2½"
			1	2½" x 11"
Red check	3	5½"	4	5½" x 10½"
			4	5½" x 5½"
Yellow check	1	1½"	4	1½" x 1½"
	2	3"	12	3" x 3"
			2	3" x 10½"
	2	2½"	1	2½" x 11"
			24	2½" x 2½"
	2	5½"	4	5½" x 5½"
			2	5½" x 15½"
Large white/red plaid	3	5½"	2	5½" x 10½"
			4	5½" x 15½"
Inner stripe border	4	1½"		
Floral border	4	6½"		
Binding (bias)	6	2½"		to equal 210"

Piecing: Center Block with Yellow Check Background

1. Make eight half-square triangles from four 3" red/yellow plaid and 3" yellow check squares. Trim to 2½".

2. Sew plaid half-square triangles and 2½" yellow check squares together in pairs. Make four. Sew plaid half-square triangles and 2½" plaid squares together in pairs. Make four.

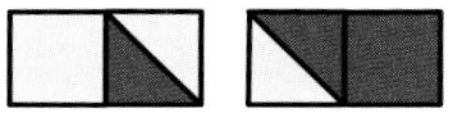

3. Sew combinations together to make a four-patch. Make four with plaid triangles facing each other as shown.

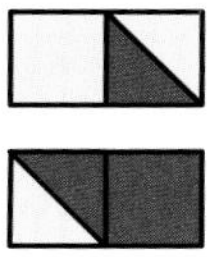

4. Sew 2½" x 11" strips of plaid and yellow check together along the long edge. Press toward the plaid. Cut at 2½" intervals. Make four cuts (2½" x 4½").

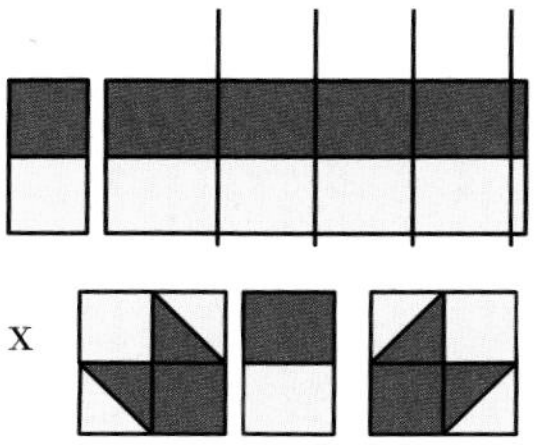

5. Arrange four-patches and strips in rows. Add a 2½" plaid square to the center row of the middle row.

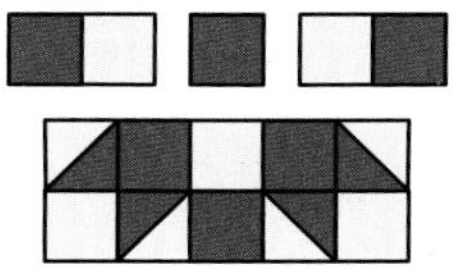

6. Sew a 3" x 10½" yellow check sashing to opposite sides of block. Press toward the sashing.

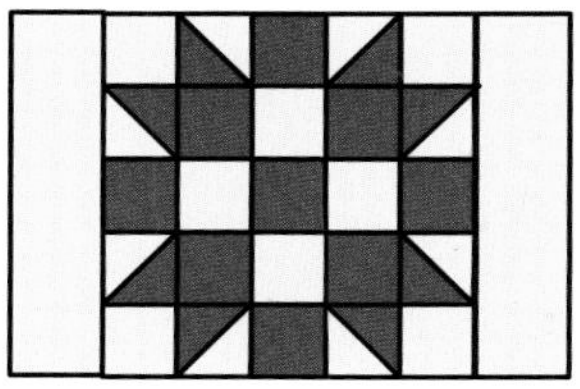

Piecing: Blocks with Red Background

1. Make 48 half-square triangles from the 3" red/yellow check and 3" red squares. Press toward the red. Trim to 2½".

2. Sew eight half-square triangles and eight red squares together  in pairs as shown. Sew eight half-squares triangles and eight red/yellow check squares together in pairs as shown. Press toward the squares.

3. Sew the pairs in rows to make a four-patch. Make eight four-patches so that the red/yellow check triangles are facing each other (4½" x 4½").

4. Sew 2½" strips of red/yellow check and red fabric together along the long edge. 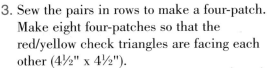 Press toward the darker fabric. Cut at 2½" intervals. Make 24 cuts (2½" x 4½").

5. Arrange four-patches and strips in rows alternating colors (eight strips will be used now). Add a red/yellow check square to the middle of the center row. Make two (10½" x 10½").

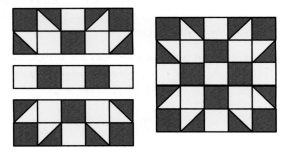

6. Sew one block to each side of the center block sashing (10½" x 15½"). Press toward the sashing.

Piecing: Blocks with Red/Yellow Check Background

1. Sew 16 half-square triangles (from Step 1) and 2½" red/yellow check squares together in pairs. Sew 16 half-square triangles and 2½" red squares together in pairs. Press toward the squares.

2. Sew pairs in rows to make a four-patch. Make 16 four-patches so that the red triangles are facing each other (4½" x 4½").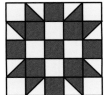

3. Sew the four-patches and strips (from Step 5) in rows, alternating colors. Add a red 2½" square to the middle row. Make four blocks (10½" x 10½").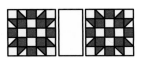

4. Sew a 5½" x 10½" white plaid rectangle between two blocks. Make two (10½" x 25½").

5. Sew a 5½" yellow check square on the diagonal to each 5½" x 10½" red check rectangle. Make two in each direction as shown.

Note: Pin in place along the seam line and turn to check angle before sewing and trimming.

6. Sew the new rectangles (from Step 4) to the ends of the blocks so that the yellow triangles point toward the corners.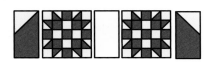

Pieced Sashing

1. Sew a 5½" red check square on the diagonal to one end of white plaid 5½" x 15½" rectangle. Make two. Note the angle of the flip corner.

2. Sew a 5½" x 15½" yellow check strip to the end of strip so that the seam is at right angles and parallel to the previously sewn square. Make two.

Note: Pin in place along the seam line and turn to check angle before sewing and trimming. Press.

3. Sew a 5½" red check square on the diagonal to one end of 5½" x 15½" plaid rectangle. Make two. Note the angle of the flip corner.

4. Sew each plaid piece to the end of the 5½" x 15½" yellow check strip (from Step 2) at right angles so that the seam is parallel to the last sewn square. Make two.

Note: Pin in place along the seam line and check the angle by turning the piece to the right side before sewing the seam and trimming.

5. Arrange and sew the center block row between the two large plaid rectangle rows.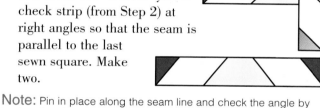

6. Sew the remaining block rows to the center section of quilt so that the yellow triangles are in the outside corners.

Border Corner Blocks

1. Make 16 half-square triangles from eight 3" yellow check squares and eight 3" red check squares. Trim to 2½".

2. Arrange and sew the 2½" yellow check squares and yellow/red half-square triangles in rows as shown. Press toward the red. Sew the rows together. Make four nine-patches (6½" x 6½").

Inner Borders

1. Measure and cut two striped inner borders the length, and two the width of the quilt top. Sew the side borders to the quilt. Press toward the border.

2. Sew a 1½" yellow check square to each end of the remaining borders. Sew to the top and bottom of the quilt. Press toward the border.

3. Measure and cut two outer borders the width, and two the length of the quilt. Sew a border to each side of the quilt. Press toward the first border.

4. Sew a pieced 6½" nine-patch block to each end of the remaining borders. Note the direction of the nine-patches. Press toward the block. Sew to the top and bottom of the quilt.

Finishing

Refer to page 12.

1. Sandwich, quilt, then bind your quilt with 2½" wide binding strips pieced to measure 210".

2. Sign and date your quilt.

Don't be afraid to mix and match your fabrics! The large floral border works well with the plaids, checks, and stripes of the Sister's Choice quilt. This variety gives your quilt interest and sparkle.

Pieced and quilted by the author
22" x 22"

Sister's Choice Pillow

This pillow is the perfect accent for the Sister's Choice Quilt.

Materials

❖ Fat quarter red
❖ Fat quarter yellow/white check
❖ ⅓ yd. red/yellow plaid
❖ 1 yd. red check for back and binding
❖ 26" x 26" batting

Cutting Directions

Red	2 squares	8" x 8"
Yellow/ White check	4 squares	3" x 3"
	4 squares	2½" x 2½"
	1 strip	2½" x 11"
	4 squares	3¾" x 3¾"
Red/Yellow Plaid	1 strip	2½" x 11"
	5 squares	2½" x 2½"
	4 squares	3" x 3"
	4 border strips	3¾" x 14½"
Red Check	2 back pieces	22" x 26"
	2½" binding strips	to equal 100"

Piecing

Review Half-Square Triangles, page 9.

1. Follow steps 1-5 for Sister's Choice Quilt (page 101) to make one block (10½" x 10½").

2. Cut the two 8" red squares diagonally once. Center the triangles on opposite sides of the block and sew in place. Press toward the large triangle. Repeat with the two remaining triangles.

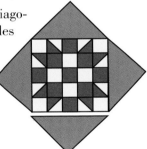

Borders

1. Sew a 3¾" plaid border strip to opposite sides of the block. Press toward the border.

2. Sew a 3¾" yellow check square at each end of the two remaining borders. Press toward the border.

3. Sew the strips to the remaining sides of the block.

4. Sandwich and quilt as desired.

Pillow Back

Review Pillow Backs, page 11

1. Fold the backing pieces in half wrong sides together to measure 22" x 13".

2. Sew a seam ⅜" from each fold to stabilize the edges.

3. Overlap the folds to equal the size of the pillow top. Lay the quilted pillow top right-side up on the back pieces. Pin the two layers together to hold the pieces while stitching around the pieces with a scant ¼" basting stitch.

4. Complete the pillow by sewing your binding of choice around the edge. Finish as you finish a quilt (see Finishing, page 12). Insert the appropriate pillow form or stuffing. Slip stitching the edge is optional.

Setting a block left from another project on point and squaring it up with large triangles makes a fun project to use as an accent in your home or to give as a gift.

Pieced by the author
Machine quilted by Bonnie Eickson
71" x 88", 14" block

Dove in the Window Quilt

As young girls, Laura and Mary had made quilt blocks from Ma's scrap bag. Now Laura was marrying Almanzo, and Ma packed Laura's "Dove in the Window" quilt to take to her new home.

Materials

- 20 plaid scraps 15" x 15" or fat quarters
- 3½" yd. background for blocks, sashing, and borders
- 4½" yd. for backing
- 1¼" yd. for binding
- 76" x 92" batting

Cutting Directions

	Number of Strips	Size to cut Strips WOF	Number of Pieces	Size of Pieces
Plaid			8	3" x 3"
			4	4½" x 4½"
			5	2½" x 2½"
Background	13	3"	160	3" x 3"
	14	2½"	80	2½" x 6½"
Sashing	8	3½"	15	3½" x 14½"
	8	3½"		
Borders	8	3½"		
Binding (bias)	9	2½"		

Piecing

Review Half-Square Triangles, page 9.

1. Make 16 half-square triangles from the 3" plaid squares and 3" background squares. Trim to 2½".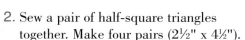

2. Sew a pair of half-square triangles together. Make four pairs (2½" x 4½").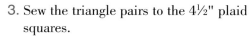

3. Sew the triangle pairs to the 4½" plaid squares.

4. Sew the remaining half-square triangles together in pairs. Add a 2½" plaid square as shown. Note the orientation of the triangles.

5. Sew the Step 4 units to the adjoining side of the plaid square to make the dove as shown.

Note: All the small triangles are pointing in the same directions.

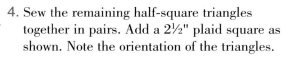

6. Arrange and sew the dove units and 2½" x 6½" background sashing strips together. Press toward the dove units. Make two for each block.

7. Sew a 2½" plaid square between two background sashing strips. Press toward the square.

8. Sew three rows together to complete the Dove in the Window. Make 20 blocks (14½" x 14½").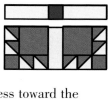

Construction

1. Arrange and sew the blocks and the vertical sashing strips (3½" x 14½") together in rows. Press toward the sashing.

2. Alternate the block rows and the pieced horizontal sashing (3½" x 65½").

3. Sew the rows together as shown.

Borders

Refer to page 12.

1. Measure and piece borders the length of the quilt top. Sew the borders to the sides of the quilt. Press toward the border.

2. Measure and piece two borders the width of the quilt. Sew the borders to the top and bottom of the quilt. Press toward the border.

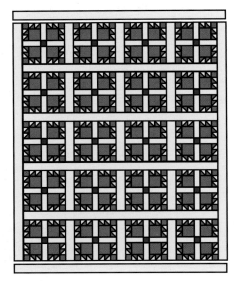

Finishing

Refer to page 12.

1. Sandwich, quilt, then bind your quilt with 2½" wide binding strips pieced to measure 330".

2. Sign and date your quilt.

The Dove in the Window block is easily adapted to smaller sizes.

Dove in the Window doll quilt (7" block)

Dove in the Window wall quilt (10½" block)

Joni Grefe made twenty 14" blue and white blocks and set them on point. She added narrow blue accent borders and wide white borders. Bonnie Erickson was quilting the quilt when Joni and three members of her family were killed in an accident. This lovely quilt belongs to Anne Grefe, Joni's daughter.

Laura tells of piecing triangles for a Bear Paw when she lived on Plum Creek. Later she takes the Dove in the Window quilt with her when she and Almanzo are married. It is interesting that the two blocks are made from the same pieces, though set together differently. Note the similarity of the blocks.

Dove in the Window (10½" block)

Bear Tracks in the Berry Patch (10½" block)

The First Four Years

Laura and Almanzo marry and move to the three room house Almanzo had built on his tree farm in South Dakota. They both work hard planting the fields but get little return from the crops. New baby Rose joins the family. After four years of crop failures, Almanzo agrees to move to apple country in Missouri, but not before they are both struck with fever from which Almanzo never fully recovers. Through it all, Laura remains optimistic.

Stitched and constructed by Beverly Keltgen
10½" x 9½"

Give Us Our Daily Bread

Laura and Almanzo chose their Christmas present from the mail order catalog. After much thought, they settled on a set of glassware that included a bread plate with the words, "Give us this day our daily bread."

Materials

- 12" x 12" background
- 4 scraps 1" x 10" for borders
- 12" x 10" for backing
- 11" x 10" batting
- Black pearl cotton

Directions

1. Trace and stitch the words (page 127) on the background fabric. After the stitching is completed, trim to 9" x 10".

2. Measure and cut two borders the length of the quilt top. Sew them to the sides of the quilt. Press toward the border.

3. Measure and cut two borders the width of the quilt. Sew them to the top and bottom of the quilt. Press toward the border.

4. Trace the wheat pattern from page 127 onto the center of the quilt top.

Finishing

Refer to page 12.

1. Place the quilt top right-side down on right side of the quilt back. Layer the batting on the wrong side of the quilt top. Stitch ¼" from the edge, leaving a 4" space to turn the quilt right-side out. Slipstitch the opening closed.

2. Quilt the wheat motif through all layers. (Pattern on page 127.)

3. Topstitch with a fancy machine stitch around the edge of the background. (Optional).

4. Sign and date your quilt.

For an alternate finish, appliqué the stitched design to a larger piece of fabric to create a larger wall hanging, place mat, or pillow.

Pieced, appliquéd, and embellished by Kathy Goral
Machine quilted by Bonnie Erickson
38" x 38", 10" block

Prairie Rose

Laura's favorite flower was the wild prairie rose that grew in great masses along the country roads. In the spring, Laura enjoyed seeing the many shades of colors and smelling their sweet fragrance.

Materials

- ❖ 1 yd. pink plaid for blocks and outer border
- ❖ ⅝ yd. green tonal for blocks and inner border
- ❖ ⅝ yd. light background
- ❖ 9" x 9" pieces pink and yellow wool or acrylic felt for flowers
- ❖ Scraps of green for leaves
- ❖ ½ yd. coordinating print for binding
- ❖ 1¼ yd. for backing
- ❖ 42" x 42" batting

Cutting Directions

	Number of Strips	Size to cut Strips WOF	Number of Pieces	Size of Pieces
Pink Plaid	4	2½"	4	2½" x 26"
			1	2½" x 13"
			4	5¾" circles
Green Tonal	6	2½"	5	2½" x 26"
			2	2½" x 13"
			2	2½" x 22"
Light	2	6½"	4	6½" x 10½"
			1	6½" x 22"
	2	2½"	1	2½" x 26"
			2	2½" x 13"
Inner border	4	1½"		
Outer border	4	3½"		
Binding (bias)	4	2½"		to equal 160"

Piecing

1. For Set A, sew 2½" x 26" strips of pink/green/light/green/pink together. Press all the seams in the same direction. Cut at 2½" intervals. Make 10 cuts (2½" x 10½").

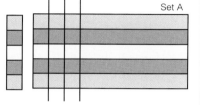

Set A

2. For Set B, sew 2½" x 26" strips of green/pink/green/pink/green together. Press all the seams in the same direction. Cut at 2½" intervals. Make 10 cuts (2½" x 10½").

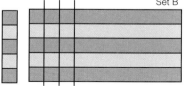

Set B

3. For Set C, sew 2½" x 13" strips of light/green/pink/green/light together. Press all the seams in the same direction. Cut at 2½" intervals. Make five cuts (2½" x 10½").

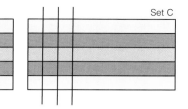

Set C

4. Arrange and sew the rows together as shown to form blocks. Make five blocks (10½" x 10½").

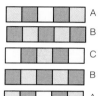

A
B
C
B
A

5. Sew a 2½" x 22" green strip to each side of a 6½" x 22" light. Cut at 2½" intervals. Make eight cuts (2½" x 10½").

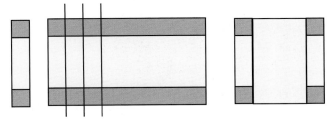

6. Sew one cut to opposite sides of a 6½" x 10½" light rectangle. Make four (10½" x 10½").

7. Arrange and sew the blocks together in rows as shown. Sew the rows together.

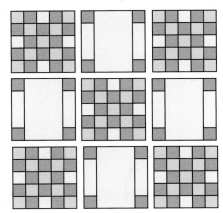

8. Appliqué circles, roses, and leaves to the light spaces using your method of choice. Embellish as desired. (Patterns are on page 119.)

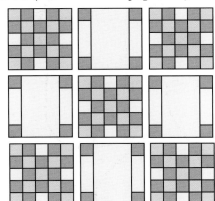

Borders

Refer to page 12.

1. Measure and cut two inner borders the length of the quilt top. Sew them to the sides of the quilt. Press toward the border.

2. Measure and cut two inner borders the width of the quilt. Sew them to the top and bottom of the quilt. Press toward the border.

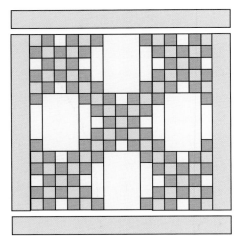

3. Repeat the sequence for the outer borders.

Finishing

Refer to page 12.

1. Sandwich, quilt, and then bind your quilt with 2½" wide binding strips pieced to measure 160".

2. Sign and date your quilt.

Laura was very fond of the lovely spring prairie rose. They are mentioned in several of the books. Laura and Almanzo named their only daughter Rose.

Pieced by Karla Schulz
Machine quilted by Bonnie Erickson
50" x 50", 9" block

Pinwheel Baby Quilt

Baby Rose's quilt is the color of the prairie roses that Laura so loved. A warmed quilt was tucked around Rose to shelter her from the cold on the trip in the cutter to Grandma and Grandpa Ingalls' house.

Materials

- ❖ 1 yd. red #1 for blocks and binding
- ❖ ¾ yd. red #2
- ❖ ¾ yd. plaid for alternate blocks, and inner border
- ❖ 1½ yd. for background, blocks, and outer border
- ❖ 2 yd. for backing
- ❖ 54" x 54" batting

Cutting Directions

	Number of Strips	Size to cut Strips WOF	Number of Pieces	Size of Pieces
Red #1-blocks	5	2½"	72	2½" x 2½"
Binding	6	2½"		to equal 230"
Red #2	1	14"	2	14" x 14"
	1	7½"	2	7½" x 7½"
	2	2½"	18	2½" x 2½"
Plaid	1	9½"	4	9½" x 9½"
Inner border	5	2½"		
Background	6	2½"	90	2½" x 2½"
	4	3½"	36	3½" x 3½"
Outer border	6	4½"		

Piecing

Review Half-Square Triangles, page 9.

1. Make 144 half-square triangles from the 2½" red #1 and background squares. Trim to 2".

2. Sew the half-square triangles together in pairs as shown. Make 72 (2" x 3½"). Sew the pairs together to make 36 pinwheel blocks from red #1 (3½" x 3½").

3. Sew a 3½" background square between two pinwheel blocks. 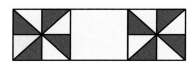 Press toward the background square. Make 18 (3½" x 9½").

4. Make 36 half-square triangles from 2½" red #2 and background squares. Trim to 2".

5. Sew the half-square triangles together in pairs as shown. Make 18 (2" x 3½"). Sew the pairs together to make nine pinwheel blocks from red #2 (3½" x 3½").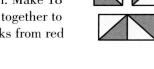

6. Sew a red #2 pinwheel block between two 3½" background squares. Press toward the background squares. Make nine (3½" x 9½").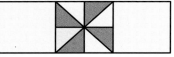

7. Arrange and sew the rows together, interlocking the seams. Make nine blocks (9½" x 9½").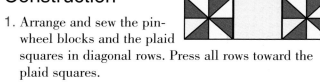

Construction

1. Arrange and sew the pinwheel blocks and the plaid squares in diagonal rows. Press all rows toward the plaid squares.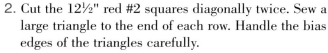

2. Cut the 12½" red #2 squares diagonally twice. Sew a large triangle to the end of each row. Handle the bias edges of the triangles carefully.

Note: Line the large triangle up at the edge of the pieced blocks so they extend beyond the outside edge. Triangles will be trimmed in Step 5.

3. Cut the 9" red #2 squares diagonally once for a total of 4 triangles. Center and sew one triangle to each corner. See Centering on page 9.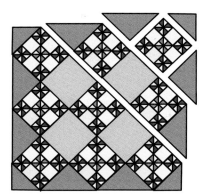

4. Press the seams in all the rows toward the plaid squares and triangles.

5. Sew the rows together, interlocking seams. Trim the outer triangles ¼" beyond the edges of the pieced blocks (38¼" x 38¼").

Borders

Refer to page 12.

1. Measure and cut two inner lengthwise borders. Sew to the sides of the quilt. Press toward the border.

2. Measure and cut two inner crosswise borders. Sew to the top and bottom of the quilt (42" x 42").

3. Repeat the sequence for the outer borders.

Finishing

Refer to page 12.

1. Sandwich, quilt, and then bind your quilt with 2½" wide binding strips pieced to measure 210".

2. Sign and date your quilt.

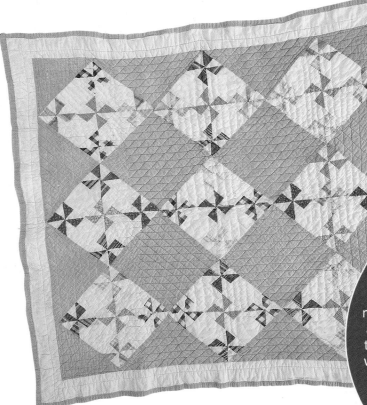

This scrappy vintage quilt was the inspiration for our Pinwheel Baby quilt. The pieced blocks are hand quilted while the alternate blocks and setting triangles are machine quilted with straight lines to create a diamond grid. The outside bias edges of the large triangles have stretched, creating wobbly borders. Our directions for cutting a large square diagonally twice should help to alleviate the problem for you. However, I do urge you to always handle bias edges carefully.

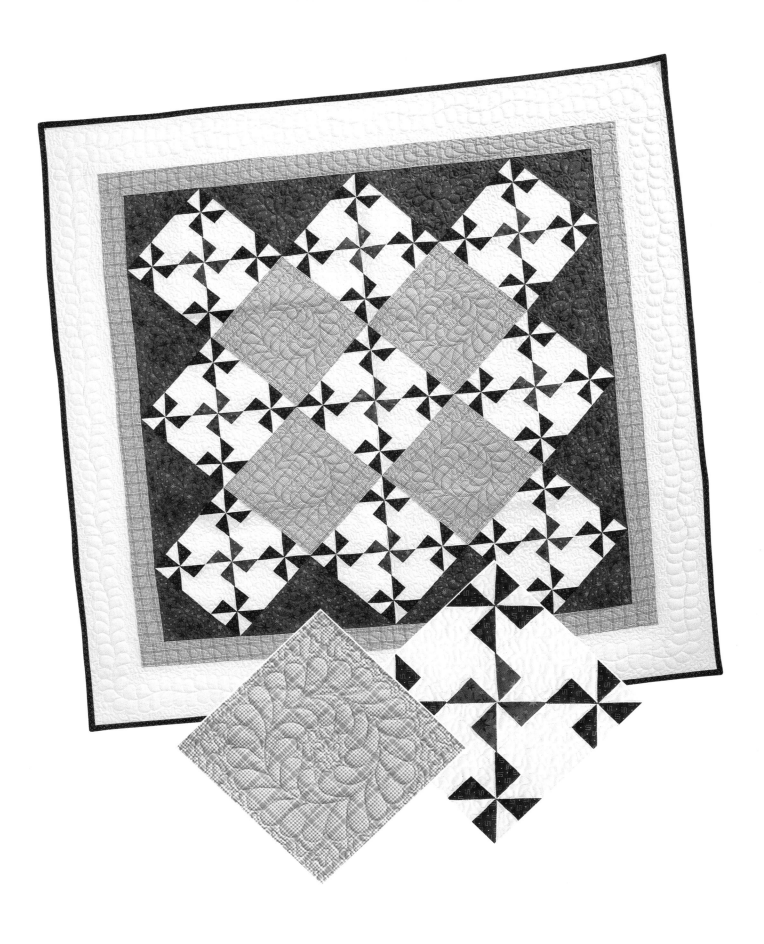

Pieced by Karla Schulz
Machine quilted by Bonnie Erickson
72" x 90"

Double Nine-Patch Irish Chain

This quilt is a replica of the Turkey red and white quilt donated by the estate of Rose Wilder to the Laura Ingalls Museum in Walnut Grove, Minnesota. The design and colors of the quilt are typical of the late 19th century when Laura was a young girl. The original quilt was pieced in double nine-patch blocks. These directions have been written to use rotary cutting tools and strip piecing methods of the twenty-first century. The original quilt has no borders as was common in Laura's day. Optional border directions are included. This version is a two-color quilt in green and tan offering an entirely different look from the original.

Materials

- 4½ yd. light fabric for blocks and background
- 3 yd. dark fabric for blocks
- 1 yd. for binding
- 4½ yd. for backing
- 74" x 94" batting
- 2 yd. for borders (Optional)

Cutting Directions

	Number of Strips	Size to cut Strips WOF	Number of Pieces	Size of Pieces
Light	35	2½"		
	5	4½"	18	4½" x 6½"
			12	4½" x 4½"
	7	6½"	31	6½" x 8½"
Dark	37	2½"		
Border (Optional)	10	6½"		
Binding	9	2½"		

Piecing: Block A

1. Sew 2½" strips of light fabric and dark fabric along the long edge. Press toward the dark fabric. Make six sets. Make 96 cuts at 2½" intervals.

2. Sew the cuts together, alternating colors, to make four-patches. Make 48 (4½" x 4½").

3. Sew 2½" strips of light fabric and dark fabric along  the long edge. Press toward the dark fabric. Make six sets. Make 48 cuts at 4½" intervals.

4. Sew a four-patch to both ends of a 4½" cut, alternating colors. Press toward the 4½" cut. Make 24 (4½" x 12½").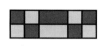

5. Sew a 4½" cut to opposite ends of each 4½" background square as shown. Press toward the dark. Make 12 (4½" x 12½").

6. Arrange and sew three sections together (two from Step 4, one from Step 5). Make 12 blocks (12½" x 12½").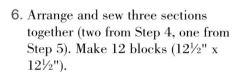

Piecing: Block B

1. Sew 2½" strips of dark/light/dark fabric together along the long edge. Make nine sets. Make 132 cuts at 2½" intervals.

2. Sew one cut to one end of a 4½" x 6½" background piece. Make 18 (6½" x 6½").

Piecing: Block C

Sew one dark/light/dark cut to each end of a 6½" x 8½" background piece. Make 31 (6½" x 12½").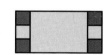

Piecing: Block D

1. Sew 2½" strips of light/dark/light fabric together along the long edge. Press toward the dark. Make seven sets. Make 76 cuts at 2½" intervals and 14 cuts at 4½".

2. Sew one 2½" light/dark/light cut to a 2½" dark/light/dark cut alternating colors. Make 28 (2½" x 6½").

3. Sew one unit from Step 2 to each end of a 4½" light/dark/light cut as shown. Make 14 (6½" x 12½").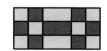

4. Sew the remaining triple combinations together to make 24 nine-patches (6½" x 6½").

Construction

1. Arrange and sew blocks together in rows following the diagram.

2. Sew the rows together.

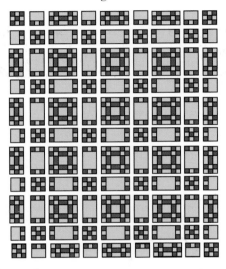

Borders

The borders on this quilt are optional. Refer to page 12 for instructions on adding borders.

Finishing

Refer to page 12.

1. Sandwich, quilt, and then bind your quilt with 2½" wide binding strips pieced to measure 335".

2. Sign and date your quilt.

This quilt, which was donated to the Laura Ingalls Wilder Museum in Walnut Grove, Minnesota, by Rose Wilder Lane, was the inspiration for our quilt. It is attributed to Laura.

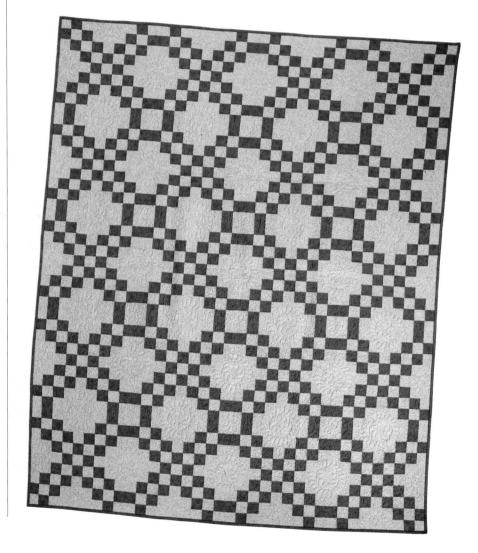